£2

Hardy Plants of Distinction

As Alan Bloom remarks in his introduction, this is not a book on new or difficult plants, rather 'Its design is to meet an awakening interest in hardy perennials, many of which have been neglected or are little known.' Certainly there could be no better informant than the author on this rich sector of ornamental gardening. Over the past thirteen years he has, at his home, Bressingham Hall, near Diss, Norfolk, created a series of beautiful gardens devoted primarily to hardy border plants, which have now become a mecca, on the numerous Open Days from spring to autumn, for gardeners from all parts of the country. In addition, Mr Bloom is head of a wholesale hardy plant and alpine nursery which is the largest of its kind in Europe.

In this book Mr Bloom gives the reader a vivid picture of distinctive hardy plants belonging to more than 80 genera, all of which he has had personal experience of growing and all of which he writes on with authority. His Merit List is a calculated assessment of the value of the plant he describes —taking into account such things as constitution, longevity, annual spread, habit, flowering season and adaptability— and his lists of plants for special purposes are also valuable to the intending planter. There is also information on the construction of 'island beds' and the conversion of conventional herbaceous borders.

The photographs included in this book illustrate how great is the diversity of interest to be found among hardy border plants—beauty of flower and leaf, gracefulness and striking habit are some of the attributes possessed by what the author is pleased to call his 'Hardy Plants of Distinction'. Plants which measure up to his critical standards are of interest to all gardening enthusiasts, and those who follow his advice can be assured of much enjoyment.

Hardy Plants
of Distinction

by ALAN BLOOM

W. H. & L. COLLINGRIDGE LTD
LONDON

First Published in 1965
by W. H. & L. Collingridge Limited
2-10 Tavistock Street, London W.C.2
Made and printed in Great Britain by
William Clowes & Sons Limited
London and Beccles
© *Alan Bloom 1965*

Contents

		Page
	Introduction	9
1	Making the most of Hardy Perennials	12
2	The Conventional Border and its Conversion	20

Descriptive Glossary of Plants

3	Acanthus, Achillea, Alchemilla, Alstroemeria, Anaphalis, Anemone, Arnebia, Artemisia, Asphodeline, Aster, Astilbe, Astrantia	27
4	Calamintha, Campanula, Centaurea, Chelone, Chrysogonum, Cimicifuga, Coreopsis, Crambe, Crocosmia, Cynara	39
5	Dicentra, Dictamnus, Dodecatheon, Epimedium, Eryngium, Eupatorium, Euphorbia	48
6	Filipendula, Gentiana, Geranium, Gypsophila, Heliopsis, Helleborus, Hemerocallis, Heuchera, Heucherella, Hosta	57
7	Incarvillea, Jurinea, Kirengeshoma, Kniphofia, Lavatera, Liatris, Ligularia, Linum, Liriope, Lychnis, Lysimachia	69
8	Macleaya, Malva, Mertensia, Morina, Oenothera, Omphalodes, Orchis, Origanum	79
9	Perovskia, Phlomis, Phlox, Phygelius, Platycodon, Polemonium, Polygonum, Potentilla, Pulmonaria	87

10 Ranunculus, Rhazya (and Amsonia), Rheum, Rodgersia,
    Roscoea, Rudbeckia, Salvia, Satureia, Scabiosa, Sedum,
    Sidalcea, Stachys, Stokesia, Thalictrum, Thermopsis,
    Tiarella, Tovara, Tricyrtis, Valeriana, Vernonia,
    Veronica   97

11 Plants for Special Purposes   111

12 Merit List and Plant Index   118

    General Index   135

Illustrations

Facing page

Island beds	16
Acanthus spinosus	17
Alchemilla mollis	17
Anemone hupehensis	17
Astrantia maxima	32
Asphodeline lutea	32
Centaurea pulchra major	32
Chelone obliqua	33
Cimicifuga racemosa Elstead Variety	33
Crocosmia masonorum	48
Eryngium alpinum	48
Euphorbia myrsinites	49
Gentiana sino-ornata	49
Geranium cinereum Ballerina	49
Helleborus orientalis	64
Hemerocallis Larksong	64
Heuchera Splendour	64
Hosta crispula	65
Hosta ventricosa	65
Kirengeshoma palmata	80
Kniphofia Springtime	80
Liatris callilepis	81
Ligularia przewalskii The Rocket	81
Liriope muscari	81
Lychnis arkwrightii	96
Macleaya cordata	96
Mertensia virginica	96
Oenothera missouriensis	97

Orchis elata   97
Phlox Norah Leigh   100
Platycodon grandiflorum   100
Rheum palmatum   101
Rodgersia podophylla   101
Rudbeckia purpurea White Lustre   108
Sedum roseum   108
Stokesia laevis   109
Veronica longifolia subsessilis hendersonii   109

Acknowledgements

My thanks to Mr A. J. Huxley for supplying the photographs of *Eryngium alpinum*, *Euphorbia myrsinites*, *Lychnis arkwrightii*, *Sedum roseum* and *Stokesia laevis*; to Mr B. Alfeiri for those of *Geranium cinereum* Ballerina and *Platycodon grandiflorum*, and to Mr H. Smith for those of *Liriope muscari* and *Mertensia virginica*.

A.B.

Introduction

This is not a book on rare and difficult plants. Its design is to meet
an awakening interest in hardy perennials, many of which have
been neglected or are too little known. In recent years perennials
or herbaceous plants have been subjected to certain pressures arising from the changing pattern of gardening. The traditional or
conventional herbaceous border, with its high rear backing and its
long sweeping vista, has revealed faults which few gardeners are
prepared to overcome. The faults are inherent in the form and
method of growing plants, and chief among them is the vast
amount of staking these borders demand. The result has been a
change-over to shrubs as a means of saving labour.

Yet some interest in perennials has remained, simply because
people found that after the spring and early summer had passed so
few shrubs could provide the colour they craved. Plant breeders
and nurserymen, ever alive to trends, as they had to be, found a
reasonable demand for such popular and mostly easy subjects
as michaelmas daisies, delphiniums, iris, lupins and phlox. Of
these, hundreds of new varieties have been introduced since World
War II which set the pattern for the labour-saving trend of the
post-war years. During these years the emphasis became so much
placed upon the popular subjects, that with their own labour diffi-
culties, nurserymen cut down their range of perennials quite
severely. Several firms existing as hardy plant specialists who, before the war, issued very comprehensive catalogues have since
dropped out simply because it did not pay.

But now the movement has begun to swing back, and this is due
to two factors. The first is the realisation that there is no satisfying
substitute for hardy perennials. Shrubs, annual flowers and bedding plants and the limited range of popular perennials which have
been dominant in recent years, cannot match the returns of a well-
balanced collection of hardy plants with their entrancing diversity
in form and colour and the vastly longer period of the year over
which they can give pleasure. The second factor to account for the

renewed interest in perennials, is due to a more rational means emerging of growing and displaying them in gardens. The conventional herbaceous border has been deeply entrenched in the minds of gardening folk for a century, but an easier, better way is at last taking on. The hedge, wall or fence at the back of the border has been the cause of lanky, weak stems that brought the need for so much staking. It has now been proved that for sturdy, erect growth, most plants need both light and air, and here the 'Island Bed' formation scores. An island bed means simply that it can be seen from all sides, which is in itself an advantage, quite apart from the fact that maintenance is reduced to the minimum.

More will be said later about island beds, how to choose and prepare a site for them and how to plan and plant. Advice is also given on how to make the best of the conventional-type border where no other site for perennials is feasible. Yet this book is not so much concerned with detailed ways and means of growing hardy plants as with bringing them to the notice of more people who yearn for variety in plants. A range of subjects is awaiting closer acquaintance in the wings, having been prevented from entry on to the gardening stage through no fault of their own.

The half dozen or so popular genera, of which so many varieties exist, have been given the limelight, along with a few well-known favourites, and my object is to beckon out the Cinderellas and describe their claims to distinction purely on their merits of garden-worthiness and individual charms. To keep within the terms implied by the title of this book, those kinds that are already well-known or popular will only be mentioned in passing or for comparison. Distinction in this sense implies not only something of striking appearance, but should rightly be also applied to charm or beauty that needs to be studied to be appreciated. The sheer blaze of colours which attracts the eye alone may be for some the criterion of beauty. For others—and these are gardeners and nature lovers in the truest sense — appreciation of beauty and charm springs from some deeper sense, appealing to the mind or heart as well as the eye.

Any appreciation of plants must, however, come down to earth. Ultimate judgment must come down firmly on the side of garden-worthiness, and this means that a plant has virtues in its favour outside all considerations of beauty and charm. Some plants are far too wild and weedy to use in a garden though they may be pretty, just as some are too fussy in their requirements to make cultivation worth while except for the connoisseur. My list will therefore be confined to subjects that are fully garden-worthy, and any faults which to my knowledge they possess will not be glossed over. In an earlier book* I devised a system of merit marks against a wide variety of plants described. Very few gained full marks because I took account of every factor of garden-worthiness: neatness of habit, long-flowering, long-living, adaptability and so on. These factors are important and will be taken into account in this book also. The plants I have described make up a list which is unconventional both in form and substance, and I should add that in spite of my 40 years as a cultivator of a wide range of hardy plants, I am still a learner. My notes are based only on what I believe I have learned so far.

*Perennials for Trouble-free Gardening (Faber & Faber).

CHAPTER ONE

Making the Most of Hardy Perennials

Any urge to make a fuller, better use of hardy perennials should be followed up firstly with some careful thought as to the purpose they are to serve. A garden is one of the few places in which we can give vent to creative self-expression. If decorative gardening appeals at all, it places us, broadly speaking, in two classes. Apart from the dwindling minority who go in for the bizarre, there are those for whom sheer display counts for most. Their satisfaction and, with luck, pride comes from massed colours in succession, and they sometimes go to a great deal of trouble to achieve this by careful planning and good cultivation. Plants, whether annuals, biennials or perennials, are used simply for the effect they produce in colour patterns, and are arranged in beds, blocks or rows just as it pleases most. It may be found fully satisfying to use such perennials as delphiniums, lupins, iris, phlox or michaelmas daisies in this way, where display is the thing, rather than to grow plants in a wide variety for their own sakes. This second class of gardener has, of course, more aesthetic leanings, and if any reader of this book is to the slightest degree conscious of this feeling, it should be fostered at the earliest possible stage, for it can lead to the deepest joys of all in gardening.

One must decide, therefore, whether to use some of the subjects I have mentioned simply to enhance display, or as a means of fostering and widening an interest in plants. If this latter be the case, then the aim should be to grow them where they will, as nearly as possible, appear to be growing in their natural home. If that garden has a damp or a shady spot then much greater scope exists for growing a wide variety of plants than if it is bare and open. But the range of plants is vast, and it would need a very large garden indeed to find a home for just those that prefer an open situation, as most of them do. The most important thing is to begin as one means, or hopes, to continue; and if there is already an unsatisfactory 'herbaceous border' of the conventional one-sided style, then the first steps may be harder to take than if only a bare site exists.

Judging from letters which I have received and conversations with visitors to my garden, many would-be enthusiasts for perennials find old conventional borders something of a problem, if not an affliction. I am often asked how a conversion from a one-sided, backed border can be made into an 'island bed', but my answer can only lead to radical changes. The backing hedge, fence or wall is usually a fixture and probably a boundary as well. A change-over must involve either a new site for perennials to some other part of the garden, or widening the border sufficiently so that it can become of island form, with a path between the backing and the bed itself. If this is impracticable then the problem might be solved by replacing the perennials with shrubs perhaps, and having an island bed carved out of the lawn in the most suitable or convenient position, or by taking in some of the kitchen or fruit garden, if that can be sanctioned. There can seldom be a solution that calls for no trouble, but it is worth considerable trouble to make a good clean beginning if there is the slightest urge to grow perennials where they can flourish, to show all the grace and beauty with which Nature endowed them. They will play their part if we first play ours by giving them a fair chance.

This does not mean that a site should always be deeply dug and heavily manured. It must be freed of all perennial weeds and quite often an old, neglected border is so infested with such weeds as couch and ground elder, along with the weedy kind of plants still in possession, that a thorough cleaning job is necessary. This may call for trenching, and I know of no major weeds apart from bindweed, thistle and marestail, that will survive if buried a foot or more below the surface. Failing this, thorough forking over during the summer when sun and wind can kill, is the best remedy, followed by careful autumn digging. Drainage is important. It should be checked if ineffective and put right, for bad drainage usually means that plants have a surfeit of moisture in the winter and early spring when they need scarcely any, and are deprived in summer when they need it most. Good drainage makes for good growth and not even moisture lovers will thrive when the soil is too wet in winter and dry or hard in summer.

A bed carved from a lawn should have the turf chopped up if it is to be buried. If it is needed for re-laying elsewhere in the garden, then it should be cut thinly so as not to deprive the new bed of the humus that topsoil usually contains. Manuring depends on the type of soil. Shallow, gravelly or chalky soils need humus added, either of compost or peat in which organic fertiliser has been mixed. Heavy clay also responds to peat or sharp sand or both, designed to make it more porous and open, kinder to till and better for root penetration. Such matters are fairly elementary and there is no need to enlarge upon these here, but advice may be needed where the selection of an island bed site is concerned. An island bed not only makes for better access, easier maintenance and stronger growth. It also provides a more pleasing setting for perennials in which they can find a home of more natural appearance if one hopes to grow a fairly wide variety of plants. There should be no hard and fast rules if this aspect is kept in mind, and both the choice of a site and its shape will emerge simply by taking careful and repeated looks from all angles as to where it will fit in best.

Environmental features must play their part, and where informal outlines of trees or shrubs permit of some informal shape, then it would be a pity to choose a formal shape for a new bed. So many gardens, however, are bounded by straight lines and to be in keeping with them a formal shape such as oval or rectangular should then be chosen. Size depends on other factors, beginning either with one's pocket or that of the garden itself. It can be as small as 10 square yards, as a midget island bed for a very small garden. There must be an upper limit, even for large gardens where funds permit, as there is still the accessibility factor. My largest bed is 40 yards long, averaging 8 yards wide, and this is only because I have the space and the plants available. It is mostly preferable to have two moderately-sized beds for better access and maintenance than one so large that a long walk is needed to get to the other side.

The choice of plants must depend on one's aims. Sometimes, when space is restricted, there may be conflict between urges for variety as opposed to display. This can be resolved by the size of the groups. Large groups containing more plants of each kind must reduce the variety in the bed as a whole and increase the display, which must also be over a shorter period. The wider the variety, in smaller groups, the more interest over the longest period but with lessened display at any one time. Single plants of a kind offer scarcely any display even if they appeal as individuals to a plant lover. I suggest that three of a kind should be the minimum number for a group even in fairly small beds, say up to 20 square yards, but a dozen of a kind would be reasonable for one of over 100 square yards. Such a matter can, however, be one of personal preference. Because I have ample scope, I am fortunate in being able to achieve both variety and display and should not try to influence readers in either one direction or the other.

A fair compromise between variety—with continuity—and display, with variations in form and colour, is within everyone's reach. This is best achieved by making a good selection of plants and, for many people, this calls for some knowledge in advance of plants from which to make a selection. The list of plants suitable for various situations which are given on pp. 111 to 117 are designed to help in this direction, in conjunction with the main descriptive text. An earlier book of mine, *Perennials for Trouble-free Gardening*, may also be helpful, although it lays no special emphasis on less-common subjects and plants of distinction.

In selecting and planning, growth-spread and habit are important. Some kinds spread five times as quickly as others, and if these are placed next to plants of slow growth, then there is likely to be trouble. Segregation is not difficult to arrange, so that plants of roughly similar growth-spread are placed in adjoining groups. This is the kind of advance information which will be helpful, and those needing it should refer to the Merit List (pp. 118 to 133) in which the number of plants to plant per square yard are specified. In island beds, the tallest plants should be placed approximately in the centre, with the shorter ones ranging down to the smallest on the outside. But lest too rigid an application of this rule leads to over-much regularity there should be groups here and there of spiky form to provide a more natural and pleasing appearance. Very few perennials have a formal appearance. Diversity in form is infinite, and the effect is best enhanced by planning with this in mind. Some kinds, especially those of the daisy family, like heleniums and asters, tend to flower on top of the stems more or less on one level. Groups of these should therefore be interspersed with spike-forming plants, some of which are most effective if they stand out boldly above or in front of their more level-headed neighbours. Kniphofias are a good example of these.

Some thought should also be given to continuity when selecting and planning. It is, of course, possible to plan beds so that the plants all flower within a period of a few weeks at any given period and still produce a harmonious, natural-looking display. But most people crave for continuity and to achieve this it is necessary to have a diversity of planting material. The first perennials usually open their flowers in March and the last are still colourful in November, with July and August as the peak months. If maximum continuity is required one may have to forgo some of those that flower in summer to make sure that there is room for those that flower in spring and autumn. Unless segregation according to season is preferred, balance is best achieved by dispersal. This means that adjoining groups should mostly contain plants which do not have flowering periods that coincide. Also, care should be taken to avoid early-flowering plants like oriental poppies (*Papaver*) and anchusa being so placed as to leave bare, unsightly gaps for the rest of the year. I have not included these plants in my descriptive glossary but if they are used then the bare gaps can be avoided by placing groups of bushy, later-flowering plants like heleniums and asters, in front of them.

Many people go to the expense of having beds or borders planned for them by professionals. Though many of the latter are my customers, I am convinced that anyone wishing to make their own plans could do so, given the kind of guidance I hope this book will provide. For some, the thought might come as a challenge, and if accepted it could prove a stimulating experience for those keen to learn more about plants. To provide the link between a given site —bearing in mind such factors as soil, climate and local environment—and a collection of hardy perennials selected to grow therein, might at first appear a formidable task, but it does not take long to find out how easily the two can be combined. Stereotyped plans such as are sometimes seen in catalogues are not for those who want to make the best use of hardy perennials. They may serve a purpose for some but for lasting satisfaction a bed or border should be planned individually to fill varying needs and situations. Such a permanent feature as a bed or border of perennials is worthy of the initial care and forethought, and worthy, too, of

Island beds in the author's garden at Bressingham Hall, Diss, Norfolk

Top left: The lilac-white flowers of *Acanthus spinosus* are guarded by sharp spikes although the leaves themselves are not prickly

Above: *Alchemilla mollis* is a low-growing plant suitable for the front of the border; it also makes good ground cover

Left: There are few late-summer-flowering plants which are as easy to grow and as charming as *Anemone hupehensis*. Its pink or white flowers are freely produced over a period of about nine or ten weeks

making the selection of plants a matter of personal choice. Ample variety exists and specialist catalogues are pretty dependable. Even if one has to spread the order to obtain all the plants desired, it is worth remembering that specialist hardy plant growers offer the best value for money. The seemingly cheapest plants may prove the dearest in the long run.

A plan need not be an elaborate affair, but it should be roughly to scale. Graph paper makes this easy and the inch squares can be used for group areas and spacings. A fairly safe average spacing works out at five plants to the square yard, but if one wishes to be meticulous the recommendations which follow can be used as a guide to variations according to spread. If one allows for groups of five plants to occupy each square yard represented by a square inch on the graph paper, planning a small- to average-sized bed or border becomes a simple matter.

Account should, of course, be taken of height and spread if one wishes to avoid troublesome maintenance in years to come resulting from harmful competition for living space. Either those plants which spread rapidly should be allowed large group spaces for the same number of plants or fewer specimens of these plants should be planted if one prefers each group to occupy a more or less uniform area. This, with the grouping together of kinds having approximately similar rates of growth spread, may take time, but a few winter evenings thus spent would be rewarding and stimulating.

Whatever space is allowed between plants within a group, it is advisable to allow extra space between the outer members of the group and those in adjoining groups. The reason for this is the promotion of strong growth which will come from light and air being allowed in and around each group. In addition, this extra space makes for easier access and minimises any risk of harmful competition.

A quite simple rule can be applied concerning the height of plants to be used. The width of a bed or border is the determining factor and some plants can spoil the whole effect if their height is too great in relation to the width of the border. The rule is — and I must admit it is one of my own making — that, when making a selection, plant heights should be restricted to half the width of the bed. This means that an 8-foot wide bed or border, island or conventional, should contain no plant exceeding 4 feet in height, and then only spike-forming plants rising above their bushier or flat-headed neighbours to break here and there any tendency to regularity. Only when the width of the border exceeds 12 or 15 feet is it safe to go in for a few well-chosen outstandingly tall subjects, especially with island beds, where the tallest are placed in the centre parts.

Foreknowledge of plants gained from a book or catalogue should provide the intending planter with useful guidance. I freely admit that in spite of a lifetime spent among plants I do not, nor will I ever, know all the answers. Height and spread often vary in differing soils and climatic conditions, and though those given have proved fairly accurate over a period of years, they are still based on my own experience as a grower. Allowance must, therefore, be made for a margin of error or misjudgment, but the home-planner need have no fears on this score. All he has to do is to make a few notes on growth rates during the first summer, and if some groups are proving to be misplaced they can easily be switched or changed with the arrival of autumn.

Autumn is the best time for planting perennials if conditions allow. Unfortunately, they are often not satisfactory. The ground may not be in a sufficiently clean, friable condition. If the wintering of freshly dug heavy soil is necessary, then it is better to wait until spring, as it is in any case if the preparation of the site and planning can only be undertaken during winter. The advantage of autumn planting is that the soil is still warm and this enables the plants to establish themselves quickly, but after mid October there is the risk of the soil being too wet or sticky. If the delivery of plants is delayed or planting cannot be carried out before such conditions prevail for some other reason, then it would be safer to heel the plants in on arrival in some well-drained spot and leave them there until conditions become favourable again in early spring. Panning through treading on wet heavy soil should be avoided and one must work with the weather to make the best use of the soil.

The conditions that make the soil too dry for safe survival are more likely to occur in early autumn or late spring. A fine spray from a good sprinkler can be applied to moisten the bed just enough — but not too much — to provide good planting conditions when the surface begins to dry off again. Failing this, puddling is the best method. Holes for each plant are filled with water and the roots are inserted after the water has soaked in. Alternatively, each plant can be inserted in the loose soil of the hole, partially covered and then well watered to draw the dry 'tilth' round the plant, the soil being firmed after the water has soaked down. It is far safer and much more effective to adopt this method when the soil is dry than a surface splash with a can or open-ended hose after planting.

CHAPTER TWO

The Conventional Border and its Conversion

So far these notes have been primarily for the guidance of those wishing to have an island bed in an open position. The needs and aspirations of those gardeners who would like to convert a conventional, one-sided border into an island bed or some compromise improvement must come next, for there are many in this frustrating position. Whether or not an improved layout can be achieved depends largely upon the width of an existing border. If it is more than 6 to 8 feet wide it may be possible to place a narrow path next to the backing hedge, wall or fence, even if this is made of pieces of paving slab laid as stepping stones. This path will, of course, reduce the width still more, but at least it has now become akin to an island bed; in most cases, however, the old bed will need a thorough overhaul. There will need to be severe restrictions on the height of plants which are used, but if, say, 3 feet is to be the limit, the tallest plants could safely be used either in the middle parts or beside the little rear path. Where an old border is quite wide — over 10 feet — then it may be possible to arrange the rear path sufficiently far away from the backing to leave a strip in which something will grow. In a mainly southerly aspect this could accommodate some slightly tender plants, perhaps bulbous, like *Nerine bowdenii*, foliage plants or others of lowly stature which prefer warm, dry conditions. If the border is on the shady side, there is plenty of choice from primroses and other dwarf, early-flowering plants.

I made two long beds on the north side of an evergreen shelter belt and rather as an experiment placed a narrow path at the rear. Beside this a strip 4 or 5 feet wide in the new bed was shady and was planted with groups of mainly spring-flowering perennials, interspersed with hostas and other shade-loving plants. This has proved a source of much pleasure and interest each year long before the rest of the bed has made much new growth. But when spring is over, then attention is focused on the other side of the beds. They are about 18 feet wide and heights range down towards the north from the tallest plants placed roughly two-thirds of the distance across. Some use can, of course, be made of the taller bushy plants to provide shade for dwarfer kinds that need it, and anyone willing to experiment on these lines may find it yields good results in gardens where shade of the right kind is lacking.

In many gardens with unthrifty or unattractive conventional borders the basic trouble is lack of width and too many tall plants. Sometimes a hard path runs beside the border, but if this consists only of gravel, it may not prove too formidable a task to dig it up and add enough width to the border to make all the difference. Such paths are often troublesome anyway, and it may well be that a lawn exists on the other side of it which will serve the same purpose as the path. Where there is no path but instead a lawn flanking the border, then it would be much easier to add to the border's width and so make the conversion into an island bed, using one's discretion as to whether the new front line is straight or curving. To achieve a pleasing effect with plants growing happily with the minimum of staking, it is of vital importance that one should make the right selection of plants. If the heights are restricted to suit the width of the bed and erect-growing kinds are chosen there need be no staking at all. The baneful effect of a backing to a border makes for weakness in plants and this is one great advantage of island beds. But there is still a fair range of plants which will stand up unaided, if one has the determination to use them exclusively to furnish a border. At a guess, at least half of the plants of 2 feet or more in height offered in most catalogues would need staking in a conventional backed border. But in island beds, as far as my experience goes, eighty per cent will stand unaided and in my own garden with nothing but island beds, well under ten per cent have to be staked.

Defined beds or borders for perennials appeal to most people, but there are other means of growing these plants. Many kinds are eminently suitable to grow in company with shrubs. Apart from the ground cover plants which are mainly used for this purpose, there are those that are fully complementary, and besides enhancing the overall effect of the border are also capable of making their own display, quite often after the shrubs have made their contribution. Such plants as kniphofias, acanthus, hemerocallis, Japanese anemones and hostas can add more than a touch of brightness and interest to plantings of trees and shrubs during late summer, when the latter have become rather drab. Where mainly deciduous flowering trees and shrubs are grown, the range of plants that provide ground cover foliage and, in most cases, flowers as well is also quite wide. A list appears on p. 117. The need for a careful selection of subjects to keep company with shrubs is just as important as it is in choosing them for any other use. Such a selection fits in well with the preferences of those who like to see plants growing as if fully at home, as if Nature intended them to be there.

This consideration comes even more into the reckoning if the facilities are available for growing woodland plants. Unfortunately, few gardens have the right kind of shade for woodlanders that dislike dry soil. The drier the shade beneath trees, the more restricted the list of plants that can be grown. Conversely, a very wide selection of plants is open to those with high shade and soil not liable to become bereft of moisture in summer. The cool, airy shade that one finds beneath tall, rather sparsely placed trees gives much greater scope than dark sites with low branches above and a mass of hungry tree roots below. A woodland garden can be a joy, with its winding paths, beside which can be grown in informal beds or plots perennials that blend to perfection with shrubs, ground cover plants, evergreens and even the trunks of the trees. The range of woodlanders is wide. The selection I have given on p. 117 is limited because not many gardens have the right conditions for growing them to perfection.

Perfection in plant cultivation is something for which true gardeners always strive. Elusive though this ideal often is, a love of plants goads us on to learn from our mistakes and always hope for success. We need sometimes to remind ourselves that the baffling or sulky plant ought not to be blamed for its lack of adaptability. If it refuses to flourish, this may well be the reason, but if we fail to give it the conditions it needs then the fault is ours. It is in the process of learning through experience and observation that we become more attached to those plants that respond to our care. If we have to give up attempts to grow some kinds that fail to respond we can be sure that others worth trying are available. My selection includes very few that, in my experience, I would call difficult or unreliable. But this is only in my experience and others may not find them so amenable. Some recommendations are proffered in this book as a means of stimulating a wider interest, with the firm belief that good use of hardy perennials brings rich rewards.

Descriptive Glossary
of Plants

CHAPTER THREE

Acanthus to Astrantia

The acanthus are nothing if not distinctive, though there are none that could be called colourful. The two most widely cultivated, *Acanthus mollis* and *A. spinosus*, have a wealth of shiny, deeply-cut leaves at the base of the plant. The word 'clump' is more applicable because once established they become quite massive, enlarging themselves from new growth arising from roots that go a long way down. I find *A. mollis* rather less hardy and less free to flower than *A. spinosus*. The latter has leaves of darker green, which, though of a prickly appearance, are not so in fact. But to grasp a flowering stem (3 to 4 feet high) will cause a swift recoil, for each hooded flower of lilac-white is guarded by a sharp spike. *A. spinosus* flowers on and off for a long period from July onwards, sometimes into November.

As natives of warmer climes, all acanthus prefer a warmish, sunny place and well-drained soil. They are drought resistant and, having nobility of form, are best in some isolation if amongst other perennials, but are valuable in company with or against a background of shrubs. The leaves of *A. longifolius* (now reckoned not to be a variant of *A. mollis*) are 18 inches long. This is nearer to *mollis* than to *spinosus* in appearance, but, with me, flowers much more freely. For collectors of out-of-the-ordinary plants, the rare *A. spinosus spinosissimus* has ground-hugging, very spiny, rather silvery leaves and occasional short spikes of flower. *A. perringii* is not prickly at all, and has big pinkish flowers on 15-inch stems, but I have found it shy to flower. All acanthus lose their leaves in winter.

Achillea
Achilleas include species that are coarse and weedy as well as some good garden plants. Some of the latter, like *Achillea filipendulina*, are common in the sense of being commonly grown,

because they are easy and useful. *A. filipendulina* grows erectly up to 5 feet or so with wide, plate heads of deep yellow and light green foliage, but here it is the dwarfer kinds I must mention. The best of these is the variety Moonshine, though in spite of knowing well enough that all achilleas like sunny open positions, I was once tempted to discard the original plant of Moonshine as being of no value. Along with a score of other seedlings it was in a row shaded by a large apple tree. One with very bright flower heads was taken out for further trial, but this failed to survive. Another was left alone when the rest were discarded, for though it had failed to flower its silvery foliage was good. There it stayed for another year until, for lack of something better, I used it to fill the last gap in a new island bed. But once divided up and planted in this open, sunny situation it began to throw flowers, and as Moonshine it has proved one of the best plants I have ever introduced. The filigree leaves are of almost year-round attraction, the plant is quite neat and very reliable and the flower heads on 20-inch stems are a glistening canary-yellow. These come into flower in early summer and odd flowers often appear later on as well.

The two parents of Moonshine are also good. *A. taygetea* is less silvery in leaf and only 18 inches tall, with early-flowering heads of a primrose-yellow shade. *A. clypeolata* makes a silvery dome of foliage topped in late summer with smallish heads of a mustardy hue. This plant will suffer sometimes from winter wet, and in spring from depredations of chaffinches, who are partial to its soft woolly leaves for nest making. Much as I admire their exquisite craftsmanship, I have to protect my group of *A. clypeolata* for a few weeks with black cotton thread.

Alchemilla

A significant change has in recent years affected people's appreciation of floral beauty. I think the flower arrangement movement initiated by Constance Spry has had something to do with it. Thirty years ago, anyone using flowers of a green hue, for example, would have been laughed to scorn. But now colour does not seem to matter, and though the rather weird green-flowered plants such as *Eryngium bromeliifolium* do not appeal to me, I can see beauty in those where green is a tinge rather than a colour. *Alchemilla mollis* is one of these where good foliage effect and masses of tiny sulphur greeny-yellow flowers combine to make a very pretty effect. As this is a dwarf plant that will grow almost anywhere and is excellent for edging or ground cover, it is surprising that it is not more widely used.

Alstroemeria

I am not quite whole-hearted in mentioning *Alstroemeria ligtu* hybrids. So many people fail to establish these tricky plants, though it should be said that once established they are there for keeps. Because of their special needs and their long dormancy they are best excluded from a mixed bed of perennials. What they like is a sheltered place, on the sunny side of a wall or with a background of evergreens, and they must have light deep soil. Established tubers send up 2½- to 3-foot stems from about 9 inches below the surface, carrying terminal clusters of very beautiful trumpet-shaped, lily-like flowers in an entrancing range of colour from palest rose to deep pink, yellow and flame-orange. But established tubers like to be left alone and will mostly languish and die if an attempt is made to dig them up, divide and transplant them. They are not difficult to raise from seed, but at every stage of growth there are hazards. Even seedlings dislike being moved and young growth is susceptible to spring frosts. A few nurserymen, having mastered the technique, offer yearling dormant tubers, and these, planted at about 6 inches deep in late summer or early autumn, stand the best chance of developing into a permanent bed.

Amsonia and Anaphalis

Because of the similarity of *Amsonia tabernaemontana* to *Rhazya orientalis* I have mentioned them together under the latter genus (see p. 98). A good deal more notice is being taken of the anaphalis. This springs partly from the search for plants with good ground cover properties that will adapt themselves to rather harsh conditions. Some ground coverers are decidedly weedy by nature and may in the long run cause a great deal of trouble, but this cannot be said of the anaphalis. All are silvery-grey and all have white or ivory flower heads of a crispy everlasting texture. There is not much to choose between *Anaphalis margaritacea*, *A. nubigena* and *A. triplinervis* except in height. The first named is about 1½ feet high in flower, when it carries a rather loose crop of branching heads.

The other two are 9 to 12 inches high and all three have the virtue of surface spread unmarred either by unsightly fading or by an aggressive weedy nature in spite of fairly rapid growth. Another virtue is that they can adapt themselves to dry places in sun or partial shade. *A. pterocaulon* is taller and more erect, and the flower heads, which are about 20 inches high, form a mat of surface growth. *A. yedoensis* dies back in winter to a spreading root system but the new shoots in spring are like silvery-white fingers. These run up to a good 2 feet making a solid bush of stems topped by papery white heads which are useful for cutting and drying.

Anemone

Anemones are too diverse for any general remarks, and only one group will be mentioned as subjects in a collection of hardy perennials that is covered by the name *hupehensis*. This is said to be correct for what was long known as *Anemone japonica* of which *hupehensis* was then a variety. But since nearly all in cultivation are garden forms or hybrids it does not really matter. No garden should be without these charming plants which can contribute so much to the late summer display. Though shades of pink and white are the only colours to be seen, it is the way their flowers are borne that makes for so much charm. Individual flowers ranging from $1\frac{1}{2}$ to $2\frac{1}{2}$ inches across remind one of the dog rose in shape, with yellow-stamened centres. From a base mass of vine-like leaves rise wiry, branching stems tipped by nodding flowers and close-set buds still to open. After a slow start in spring, most varieties begin flowering in late July or early August and will continue until autumn has set in. Ten weeks is a long flowering season for any plant and this, added to overall grace of habit, plus inherent longevity and adaptability, leaves little to be desired. Good drainage and a mainly sunny position are the only essentials to cultivation and they are especially good on chalky soil.

The tallest varieties are white, and Louise Uhink has rather larger flowers than Whirlwind, both reaching about $3\frac{1}{2}$ feet. There is little to choose between some of the single pink varieties such as Queen Charlotte, Max Vogel and Kriemhilde, which are all about $2\frac{1}{2}$ feet high. The semi-double Montrose and the near double Lady Mary Gilmour are much dwarfer, as are the deeper rose-pink Profusion and Bressingham Glow. These are only 20 inches tall and the latter is neat of growth and warm of colour. A few varieties linger under the name of *hupehensis*, denoting a rather more spreading type of growth — very dainty and with smaller flowers. *A. hupehensis splendens* or *superba* are about 18 inches in height but September Charm is taller. One word of advice: old plants are slow to recover if lifted and divided, and young pot-grown stock are the best investment. One other anemone is worth a mention. It is the hybrid *A. lesseri*, a plant that likes a fairly moist and not too sunny a place. What it lacks in robustness it makes up for in beauty and in May and June the glowing rosy-red flowers on erect 18-inch stems are most attractive. This is a choice plant for those who can give it the treatment it needs and deserves, and though it lacks a vigorous spread, it is reliably hardy and perennial.

Arnebia and Asphodeline
Plants are usually rare either because they are difficult to grow or because they are simply not well enough known and therefore exist only here and there in gardens and nurseries. A nurseryman's job should include the gentle exploitation of good but little known plants. It is good business to do so, provided his judgment is sound. If he can propagate and show something out of the ordinary or an improvement of an existing kind, then the gardening public will buy.

Arnebia echioides is not an improved variety, but is virtually the only species of arnebia in cultivation in Britain. It has, in fact, been in cultivation for many years but what astonishes me is that it is still very rare. It is an outstanding example of a 'Cinderella' plant and having found it quite easy to grow for the past 12 years, there is no valid reason why it should be so rare, especially as it is so beautiful. *A. echioides* belongs to the borage family and has the characteristic rough tongue-shaped leaves of a bright green hue. These come from compact crowns, to make a dense tuft, and below are black fleshy roots. In spring come little sprays of pure yellow flowers of anchusa shape, and where each of the five petals join there are five deep maroon spots. These fade out later but they are responsible for the plant's common name of Prophet Flower. Legend has it that Mahomet on a journey tripped up but a plant of arnebia cushioned his outstretched hand as he fell forward. The five spots are the imprints of the prophet's fingers. Flowering begins in April and lasts for a month or more; the flowering stems never exceed about 10 inches, and often throw odd sprays of flowers at intervals until autumn. Its only needs seem to be a mainly sunny position and reasonably good, well-drained soil. The time must be near when some exhibitor at Chelsea Flower Show will make a splash with this fine little plant and so make it better known to the gardening public.

In somewhat the same category, though with a different appeal, is *Asphodeline liburnica*, or, as it is sometimes called, *Asphodelus liburnicus*. *A. lutea* is not so uncommon with its tapering spikes 4 feet or so tall, on which yellow flowers come and go for many weeks. It is a statuesque kind of plant with glaucous foliage like narrow drooping straps, and it is quite easy to grow in a sunny position and ordinary soil. *A. liburnica* is of similar habit but is more compact as a plant and more graceful in appearance. The stems are willowy and the foliage much finer, grey-green and grassy, both along the slender 3 to 4 feet stems and around the base of the plant. The flowers are golden-yellow and though quite small-petalled, they hug the stems for most of its length and give a long if subdued display. The root is hardy, adaptable and long-lived, and most people who have seen it growing at Bressingham are attracted, as I am, by its charm as a flowering plant.

Artemisia

The artemisias are adaptable, though a dryish sunny place brings out the best foliage effect. There are a dozen or so species, all silver-leaved, but some need curbing lest they invade neighbouring groups. This danger is present with *Artemisia ludoviciana*, *A. palmeri*, *A. pontica*, *A. purshiana* and *A. baumgartenii* (*syn. A. villarsii*), all of which are rather better placed both for effect and expedience in front of shrubs and evergreens. Among other perennials the group would need to be curbed annually by forking out excessive growth. The flowers are scarcely worthy of description and the plant at a distance is of more or less uniform colour. *A. stelleriana* is rampant, but only on the surface. It has little value unless consolidated by replanting every year. *A. argentea*, *A. discolor* and *A. splendens* are pretty with silver filigree foliage and are slightly more shrubby in growth and less rampant. I find they need tidying up

Right: The scabious-like astrantias are light pink and this species, *A. maxima*, has the largest flowers

Above: *Asphodeline lutea*, with its yellow flowers and strap-like leaves, is a plant which deserves to be seen more often than it is, particularly as it is hardy and long lived

Right: The deep pink heads of *Centaurea pulchra major* are fully 3 inches across, borne on top of stiff straight stems 1½ to 2 feet tall

Left: *Chelone obliqua* has hooded flowers of rosy-magenta, which appear in August, and it is closely related to the penstemon

Below: The feathery white bottle-brush flowers of *Cimicifuga racemosa* Elstead Variety are extremely distinctive, and the plant grows well in partial shade

every spring, however, because they lack compactness of growth. The one silvery species which in my garden is compact, with good foliage, and which, in short, has real distinction, is *A. nutans*. From a tough woody rootstock come ample, erect, wiry stems to about 2 feet and the effect of the whole plant is a graceful bush, attractive in all stages of growth from May to October. This is a plant without a vice, and in well-drained soil and sun will keep its attraction for several years.

With one exception all the artemisias mentioned are best in sun and are better on poor dry soil than rich. The exception is *A. lactiflora* and this is as distinct as it is distinctive. It is entirely herbaceous, making a clumpy plant that retains over winter a tuft of green leaves like Sheep's Parsley. In summer come strong stems well clothed in greenery, until by late August they are over 4 feet high and plumed with ivory-cream. If this fades too quickly or the leaves go brown too soon it is because the soil is too poor or dry, for this plant responds to moisture and good soil. And if, after three or four years, an old clump dies out in its centre parts, it is time to transplant the still lively outside pieces into freshly dug and enriched ground.

Aster

The genus *Aster* includes Michaelmas Daisies of various types. With a welter of named varieties it is not surprising that a few of the species are suffering from undeserved neglect. But an aster is an aster and claims to distinction can only be based on garden value. *Aster acris*, for example, is a first rate plant with its myriads of starry blue flowers on dense bushes $2\frac{1}{2}$ feet high in August and September. It is a neat-growing plant and calls for no staking as do many of the taller kinds. There is a dwarfer form, *A. acris nanus*, which can be really effective in a frontal group, but one of the most appealing of dwarf kinds is *A. thomsonii*. Even in the fairly rich Bressingham soil, it never exceeds 18 inches high, with 1-inch wide blue, yellow-centred flowers above erect grey-green growth. This begins to flower in July and continues until October without loss of beauty. It is one of those plants that possesses the ability to sustain a long flowering period from resources one would scarcely expect, considering its slow rate of expansion as a plant. It is hardy enough, but none-the-less comes into the category of choice plants never likely to become common through over-production. This, by the way, is one of the parents of that sterling hybrid *A. frikartii*. Its other parent is *A. amellus* and strangely enough *frikartii* is taller, at 3 feet, than either. What is even more remarkable about *A. frikartii* is that the larger flowers of *A. amellus* have combined with the long flowering season of *A. thomsonii*.

Another uncommon aster worth mentioning is the stiffly bushy *A. laevis*. This grows to 2½ feet and bears starry lilac-coloured flowers in July and August. Then there is the 18-inch *A. spectabilis* which gives sprays of rich violet, orange-centred flowers an inch across from August to October. Both are easy to grow and the latter makes quite a mat of dark green leaves. The slender-leaved, wiry-stemmed *A. linosyris* is deep yellow, the flowers being carried on a terminal head like a bunch of little puffs. This species is August flowering, and a variant named Goldcrest is a little later and a trifle more graceful. For grace, as a change from the sheer spectacle of the modern varieties of Michaelmas Daisy, the *cordifolius* asters have it. These are available from some nurseries in shades of light blue and silvery-lilac and though small-flowered are quite charming with their long sprays 3 to 4 feet tall.

Astilbe

Astilbes grown in good soil with adequate moisture achieve perfection from every point of view as plants of incomparable beauty. Attractive wide-based foliage often mounds up to a shapely pyramid formation through which the plumed spike appears. These spikes are of every imaginable shade from white through pink, salmon and cerise to fiery red and deep red. Some are erect, others arch and droop, and heights vary from 6 inches to 6 feet. None ever need staking and as plants they are completely hardy and can be left alone for years, trouble-free and reliable, though they cannot stand hot, dry conditions. Many varieties are quite safe where soil is reasonably good and does not bake, but for perfection, they need moisture and will last in flower longest away from strong sun and parching winds. They respond heartily to mulching in spring, which, of course, conserves moisture, but during a drought moisture given by any means is so rewarding that any trouble taken to do this is worth while.

With astilbes it is a case of not allowing them to dry out, and it is ample moisture and richness of soil, together with shade, that brings a full reward. Planting is safe at any time between October and April, for the solid, somewhat woody-crowned plants are fairly late to begin new growth. Old plants of the stronger kinds may become quite massive, but if replanting ever becomes necessary then all one has to do is to break up the crowns into manageable pieces and to discard the older, more woody growth in the centre and lower parts. In general, the tallest growing astilbes are the strongest and least fussy about moisture, but these do not include the brightest colours. One of the best of the taller kinds is *Astilbe taquetii superba*, with imposing spikes, straight and strong, of an intense lilac-purple shade. This variety averages about 4 feet in height and is at its best in July and August. *A. davidii* and the varieties Tamarix, Salland, Venus and Salmon Queen are all quite tall and very robust with colours ranging from the pale pink of Venus to the lilac-rose of *davidii*. The tallest astilbe with me is *A. rivularis*. This sends up stout stems to 5 or 6 feet, with ample foliage and fine arching plumes of creamy-white in August. *A. astilboides* is more compact in root and shape and the more erect plumes come a month earlier in July. Both of these show some resemblance to the June-flowering *Aruncus sylvester*, which for all practical purposes comes into the same category for use and cultivation. All three, unfortunately, have an all too brief season. When their plumes pass their majestic zenith rusty fading mars their beauty.

Given the right conditions, the more colourful range of dwarfer astilbes will provide a much longer flowering period. These are hybrids, mostly of Continental origin, growing from $1\frac{1}{2}$ to 3 feet tall and flowering between late June and mid-August. There are at least 40 varieties in cultivation and some of the older varieties one still sees cannot bear comparison with those of more recent introduction. Some of these are named after German cities by the raiser, Herr Arends, whose nursery is perched 900 feet up on the hills above Wupperthal. Coblence, an early rich carmine-red; Bonn, a bright rose-pink; Cologne, deep carmine-rose; and Dusseldorf, salmon-pink, are all about 2 feet high. So are Rheinland, early, clear pink, and Deutschland, a fine white. For reds of this height, Fire is a very intense shade, and Red Sentinel is almost brick-red. It lacks vigour, however, but Glow, at $2\frac{1}{2}$ feet, is stronger and

Spinell is another fiery shade. The 2½-foot Federsee is a rosy-red variety which seems able to tolerate drier conditions than most, as does Bressingham Beauty with fine clear pink spikes. The orchid pink Cattleya is another strong grower; Ostrich Plume is of quite distinctive form, and the clear pink Finale is fairly late to flower. Fanal is a deep red dwarf variety, barely 2 feet high, and another white variety of rare charm with dark green leaves is Irrlicht. The deeply divided foliage makes a big contribution to the beauty of astilbes and there is infinite variation in the shades of green to be found among them, including some of bronzy and purplish hue. In the quite dwarf variations of *A. simplicifolia* the leaves are prettily varnished, overlapping one another in mound formation above which come sprays, rather than spikes, of flowers. *A. simplicifolia atro-rosea* has bushy sprays of bright pink 15 inches high, but the dainty Bronze Elegance — the bronze refers to the foliage — is clear rose and only 9 inches high. Dunkelachs, with erect salmon-pink spikes, is another little beauty, though not so robust. The foliage shows further variation in the one or two *crispa* variations of astilbe which have dark green leaves of crinkly crispness. Perkeo has pink poker spikes 6 to 9 inches high. One fairly robust dwarf which will spread quite quickly where it is moist is *A. chinensis pumila* (*A. sinensis pumila*) with soil-hugging foliage and dumpy 10-inch spikes of light purple. For daintiness, the miniature *A. glaberrima saxosa* is quite charming. It is only 4 or 5 inches high and the colour is pale pink. In habit it is a perfect miniature, but it must have shade and moisture. This, of course, is in keeping with my generalisation that the dwarfest astilbes are the most demanding of the cool moisture with abundant humus in which astilbes revel.

Astrantia

The astrantias have mostly a greeny tinge in their flowers and are a good example of how many people no longer spurn plants in which colours are subdued. In my early days as a producer of plants there was no demand whatever for any of the astrantias, but it is a very different story now. Only a few species are in cultivation and in the most extensive catalogue one is not likely to see more than three listed. The commonest is *Astrantia major*, sometimes listed as *A. carniolica major*, a vigorous growing plant with flower stems reaching a height of about 2½ feet. The flowers, barely an inch across, and carried as a loose flattish head, are very delicately petalled, whitish with a tinge of pink as well as green, and with a pretty centre tuft of upstanding stamens of the same hue. I have heard some old diehards call this a dirty colour, but what it lacks in brilliance it makes up for in charm, when one looks at it closely. Growth is of a fairly robust mat formation and the leaves — light green and deeply cut — are typical of its family, the *Umbelliferae*. In moist soil it is apt to be a little invasive, but is easily curbed. *A. rubra*, which may be a form of *carniolica*, is far from being invasive and is best grown where not too dry and sunny. Leaves of this are mounded and dark green and the flowers are borne in heads only 12 inches high. The colour is a very subdued dark red in which green is scarcely noticeable, though it may account for the lack of brilliance. In spite of this, it attracts to the extent of making it a scarce plant. To my mind, the most attractive astrantia is *A. maxima* (*A. helleborifolia*) to which the Royal Horticultural Society gave an award of Merit in 1964. It is as tall, and in moist soil a little taller, than *A. major* and the flowers are larger, of a distinctive and very charming shade of light pink that glistens in the sun. Astrantias seldom need supporting though I have known them to flop somewhat when heavy rain and wind have been experienced when they are in full flower.

Letting Off Steam

I sometimes have rebellious feelings when, at the behest of botanical authorities, a well-known plant name has to be changed. Some of these people seem to live in a world of their own and make their pronouncements with utter disdain for common usage in nomenclature. Botanical names are very necessary, and we would soon be in a hopeless muddle if any attempt were made to dispense with them. But where a plant name has been used and accepted for a long time, it should not be changed except for the best of reasons. There must be far more people who have to use plant names as horticulturists than as botanists, and the latter must not be surprised if the horticulturists tend more and more to stick to common usage as the only means of avoiding endless confusion. There are cases where some members of a particular genus have been given separate generic status, such as *Ligularia* as distinct from *Senecio*, while others have been merged — for example *Betonica*, which is now included with *Stachys*. This last would appear to make for simplification, but my reason for letting off a little steam at this point is that two good plants I intended describing now have been transferred to another place alphabetically. Since they are at least becoming accepted after many years as *Macleaya* and *Stachys* rather than *Bocconia* and *Betonica*, the changes ought to be conceded. It is future changes that ought from now on to be resisted, when they make for complication rather than simplification.

CHAPTER FOUR

Calamintha to Cynara

Since my garden was allowed to settle down, as it were, I have been better able to assess the qualities of some of the lesser-known plants it contains. From 1957 to 1963, so much was added both in area and variety that many subjects were moved too frequently to become fully established, but in any case it is safer to judge a plant on a long-term performance. One can form an opinion in one season that may have to be changed the next, or even during the one after that.

Among those that have proved both reliable and attractive is *Calamintha nepetoides*. It is not so much like a catmint as its name implies and though it grows about the same height as the ubiquitous *Nepeta mussinii* it is much less sprawling and the flowers are larger, blue and white combining to provide a decidedly airy effect. It grows happily in partial shade, is of moderate spread, and apart from being long lived has an exceptionally long flowering period from July onwards. As an easy to grow, deep pink-flowered calamintha, *grandiflora* has some merit. Though by no means eye-catching, it flowers unobtrusively for many weeks. It is best grown in a place which is not too dry or sunny. These calaminthas belong to the mint family and have slightly aromatic leaves.

Campanula

One of my earliest collecting urges was centred on campanulas. Thirty years ago the conflict between growing plants for love and the need to make a living by growing them for profit inevitably meant coming down on the side of the latter. All the same, I had almost furtively accumulated 109 species and varieties of campanula before the nurseryman in me took control. And rightly so, because I was well under thirty and had not long before embarked on my own account with ambitions greatly in excess of experience and capital. Campanulas have never ceased to be one of my

favourite genera, from the dainty alpine harebells to the tallest
border kinds. Now there are probably more than 109 species and
varieties in my garden, but only a few of the most outstanding
can be mentioned and these must exclude rock garden types. I
should qualify this, however, because so many dwarf campanulas
usually seen in rock gardens are very effective as frontal border
groups. Height in plants is only one aspect of suitability and
adaptability. Campanulas that are constitutionally robust are
adaptable for both border and rock garden even though they may be
only a few inches tall when in flower. *Campanula carpatica* in
variety vary from 6 to 12 inches in height, and are a good example
of dual-purpose plants.

This preliminary prompts another. Among last year's visiting
nurserymen was one who, on seeing a group of *C. lactiflora* in the
garden, asked if I had heard about a new dwarf version of this
sterling plant. He went on to describe how, instead of running up
to form sprays of pale lavender-blue bells on 3-foot stems, it
hugged the ground like cushions on which the same sized flowers
sat. Decidedly intrigued, I asked for the name of the new variety
but when he replied that it was rather aptly named Pouffe I had to
give a very broad grin. When I told him that I had raised and named
Pouffe in 1935, he was at a loss to know how it was he imagined
it was new in 1963. So was I. It was his first visit, but the plant
had been listed in my catalogue, which he had received every
year since 1937.

No doubt this was more of an oversight on his part since Pouffe
has been distributed, even if it has taken a long time to become
accepted. I can claim no credit for raising such a plant. It simply
appeared as a midget edition in a batch of seedlings, having the
attractively freakish habit of spreading outwards rather than upwards, thereby making an excellent subject for a frontal group
and even for certain positions in the rock garden.

Many campanulas are quite at home in partial shade and *C.
lactiflora* in all its forms is among these. Left alone they will naturalise
from self-sown seed, especially in semi-shady places. They
are of graceful growth, have light green leaves and flowers in
shades from pale lavender-blue to the deep blue of Prichard's
Variety. This is a very good plant, 2½ feet tall as compared with
the more usual 3½ feet and the 5 feet of the pale pink Loddon Anna,

which is very robust and quite striking. With all of them, flowering begins in late June and ends in August, but Pouffe holds out for longest.

Campanula alliariifolia has ivory-white bells on arching stems about 20 inches long. It is a pretty plant that prefers sun and grows just as well in inhospitable gravelly soil as in soil which is rich and moist. But it seeds itself too freely, as do many plants that are by nature rather short lived. However, the similar *C. alata* (the name is at present being disputed) is fully perennial and a more desirable plant. It forms a fairly hefty clump, mounded with softly hairy leaves of a slightly greyish tinge, like those of *C. alliariifolia*, and the sprays of thimble-sized white bells dangle from 18-inch stems during June and July. This is a very pleasing plant and one which ought to be better known. *Campanula latifolia* is another capable of seeding itself, but is none the less long lived. It has erect stems a good 3 feet tall with quite large, pointed-petalled bells. The best known is the violet-coloured Brantwood, but there is a pretty white flowered variation, as well as one called Gloaming, of the palest mauve-blue imaginable. The flowers have an opaque quality which I find most attactive. *C. latifolia* prefers soil which is not too dry and if it has some shade will last longer in flower. Its only fault is that it has rather a brief season when grown under dry conditions.

Campanula glomerata has several variations. Some of them have a creeping rootstock which can be a nuisance if neglected, especially in *C. g. dahurica*, the variety most often seen, which produces too few of its 2-foot heads of clustered violet-purple flowers. The true *C. g. superba* is better, though taller, but the little Joan Elliott is reliable. It flowers freely, the richly coloured bells on 15-inch stems first appearing in late May. *C. g. acaulis* bears stumpy spikes in June and July, up to 18 inches high, in deep blue, white and an intermediate shade which is called *lilacina*. Then there is the newly introduced Purple Pixie which I find difficult to believe belongs to *C. glomerata*. This does not flower until well after the others have finished and has little resemblance to it in form. A neat tuft produces stiff but shapely pyramidal spikes up to about 15 inches in height in late July and August.

Campanula Percy Piper has shining, deep blue saucers clasping most of the 3-foot spike, coming from a bright green mat of foliage. This is a hybrid with most kinship to *C. latiloba* and it makes a very bright display in June and July. It is a reliably easy, long-lived plant.

An old variety of the nettle-leaved *C. trachelium* deserves a mention. It is Bernice, neat of growth, with upstanding 2-foot stems carrying large, double, powder-blue flowers in June and July. *C. burghaltii* is seldom seen, though it is easy to grow. The stems are a trifle spindly and lax, 18 inches tall, but they carry disproportionately large drooping bells of a pale smoky-blue shade for several weeks. Of similar growth *C.* Van Houttei is deeper blue, and both have an appeal to the many where oddity is combined with a certain degree of charm.

Centaurea

Knapweed is the common name for wild centaurea, which is native to Britain. Some species native to other countries, brought to Britain, have proved of a rather weedy nature, with little more garden worthiness than our own. But there are some centaureas well worth a place including one or two that are quite choice. In general, centaureas are easy to grow, much preferring sun and dry, rather than moist, soil. The two most frequently seen in gardens are certainly not the best either from the habit and growth point of view or from the flowers they bear. *Centaurea montana* is one of these, a dwarf but floppy grower producing single petal-deficient flowers in May and June of pink, violet or mauve. *C. montana* spreads quickly, and though the other, *C. dealbata*, is less of a spreader, it makes an excessively large plant and becomes so starved that the pinkish cornflower-style flowers fail to keep pace. *C. dealbata steenbergii* is equally robust, but the flowers are larger, of a more pleasing pink shade; easily the best of this type is the newer John Coutts with fine large pink flowers in June and July from leafy grey-green plants. All three are about 2 feet tall.

Centaurea glastifolia is taller, with 4-foot stems, carrying canary yellow puffs. The leaves are greyish and the plant has something distinctive about it, though it is less striking than *C. macrocephala*. This is quite a giant and the garish yellow puffs are round and large as tennis balls. The leaves, too, are large and light green. Both species have deep fleshy roots, and to dig up an old plant of *C. macrocephala* would call for much exertion. The most graceful of this type is *C. ruthenica*, for its 4- to 5-foot stems are slender and branching. The leaves are deep green, finely cut and shiny. All flower in June and July.

There are three little known species, sufficiently dwarf, neat and attractive to use as frontal groups. The smallest is *C. simplicicaulis*, having deep pink flowers on wiry 9-inch stems above rosettes of greyish leaves. My preference, however, is for *C. hypoleuca*, for it has good grey foliage in dense clumps and the light pink flowers of cornflower type keep coming for many weeks from early June onwards, but their stems are only 12 inches tall. The third is *C. orientalis* (*C. rigidifolia*), again grey leaved and pink flowered and not lacking in robustness. This reaches 18 inches and, like the other two, retains its foliage over winter.

The real aristocrat amongst centaureas is surely *C. pulchra major*. From a stout fleshy root comes an abundance of handsome wide-spreading leaves of greyish hue. Straight as a ramrod comes up a stem $1\frac{1}{2}$ to 2 feet tall topped by a gorgeous deep pink head 3 inches across. This is a plant that needs to be in some isolation for full effect and it also prefers to stay put, as it will for many years without deterioration. I have a particular affection for this plant, apart from its beauty. Before 1939 I slowly built up a stock to about 50 plants, but, through the hazards and losses of the war years, there was only one piece, half dead, to bring when I moved to Bressingham in 1946. The nursing process then began all over again and now at last I have established plants to delight my eye. One reason for the losses was enforced neglect during the three hard winters of the 1940s and from this I learned that the best position is in deep, open soil facing the sun and backed by evergreens or a wall.

Chelone

The chelones are quite close relatives of the penstemon. Indeed *Chelone barbata* is often classified as such, to which it has more resemblance than other chelones. These do not have open-ended tubular flowers as do penstemons, but in the very distinctive *C. obliqua* they are like blobs of rosy-magenta hugging the leafy 2-foot stem. The plant has a creeping rootstock with tough underground shoots to form a slowly expanding mat. After winter dormancy, up come stiff stems with deep green pointed leaves, until by August they are well in flower, staying colourful for several weeks. It may not be everyone's colour but it is a showy plant, much more pleasing than the more spindly white form *C. obliqua alba* (correctly *C. glabra*). *C. lyonii* makes a lowly but dense bush about 12 inches high of very short spikes of suffused white, pink and purplish blobs. This too is quite accommodating and quite attractive in a subdued way; both prefer a sunny place.

Chrysogonum
Full marks go to *Chrysogonum virginianum* for longevity and long flowering. With me, the little golden four-petalled flowers continue unceasingly from May to October, nestling as 6- to 8-inch sprays amid light green leaves. This is a dual purpose plant for the rock garden or the front of the border, with only a dislike of lime in the soil to mar adaptability to all situations where a reliable dwarf plant is needed. Yet one seldom sees it, even in lime-free gardens, and one can only wonder why it has been so long neglected.

Cimicifuga
Translated from Latin to English, cimicifuga gives the common name of bugbane, but this is strictly applicable only to *Cimicifuga foetida* or the Stinking Bugbane. Such a preamble might be a bane to gardeners, too, but some of the cimicifugas in cultivation are very desirable subjects indeed. Showing little resemblance to other members of the buttercup family, all have slender, graceful spikes of tiny pearl-white flowers, varying in height from 3 to 7 feet and in season from late July to October. To achieve the perfection in form of which they are capable, the soil must not be dry or hungry, and though not objecting to full sun where these essentials are met, they are partial to some shade. The roots are clumpy and fibrous and the plants are very long living; and though new growth in spring is tardy, even the latest to flower create a good foliage effect with flower spike formation well-developed long in advance of the opening time of the slender bottle-brush terminals.

   Cimicifuga cordifolia with creamy-white flower spikes, in August and September, is very slender and reaches little more than 3 feet. *C. dahurica*, not often seen, is a little taller with more conspicuous flowers. *C. japonica* spreads its deeply cut foliage more widely and has fairly thick white pokers, reaching a height of 5 feet where suited. *C. racemosa*, best in the varieties White Pearl or Elstead Variety, is late flowering and very effective when even Michaelmas Daisies are fading. The tallest, *C. ramosa*, comes in September with strong 7-foot branching stems and tapering pokers of creamy-white. All are very good value and very distinctive in the conditions they like, but even if afflicted by drought in one season they will respond the next with undiminished vigour to more normal rainfall.

Coreopsis

Specialists in almost any field tend to disdain the ordinary, as knowledge and, perhaps a collection, increases. Coreopsis are among the ordinary plants which might well be passed over in a book about plants of distinction. But at least one coreopsis is good and so rewarding in spite of its easy growth that it merits inclusion. It is *Coreopsis verticillata*, which in all respects but its colour is very distinct from any other. When not left too long in one place so that it becomes starved, plants of *C. verticillata* develop as the thin purplish-green shoots rise from winter dormancy into bushes of deep green barely 2 feet high. From about midsummer to September these bushes are constantly decked with starry yellow flowers 1½ inches across. There is also a slightly taller, slightly deeper yellow variation named *C. v. grandiflora* and one or the other would be included if I were asked to suggest a list of a dozen best border plants.

The most common coreopsis but certainly not to be despised are those of *C. grandiflora* or *C. lanceolata* breed. Most of them are short lived, though easily raised from seed, providing a long succession of deep yellow flowers on rather weak stems. Of recent introduction from Germany are some midget variations. One named Goldfink is only 6 or 8 inches high, rounded in habit and erect in flower. This is bright yellow and another, Rotkichlen, has brown zonings at the base of each petal. So far they appear to be fairly good perennials but this test, especially when up against the British climate, needs to cover several seasons. All these types of coreopsis have considerable growth above the surface and comparatively little by way of below-ground rootstock, and it is the vitality and durability of the latter that decides the degree of the plant's hardy perennial nature. There is a little-known coreopsis with very fragile roots, *C. rosea*, but these roots still have this vitality necessary to carry the plant through winter after winter. It bears small, very pale pink flowers in late summer and autumn and is pretty but by no means striking. It is only 9 inches high and has tiny narrow leaves. The roots are a mass of tiny rhizomes and in dampish soil capable of spreading into pretty solid mats.

Crambe

Crambe cordifolia is a massive plant and this has a closely related edible vegetable in sea kale (*C. maritima*). *C. cordifolia* makes a huge fleshy root with woody crowns above the soil and much more below. In spring, shoots quickly rise to form broad heart-shaped, horse-radish type leaves and widely branching stems up to 6 feet high. In late May and June these carry countless white flowers, four-petalled and of shilling size in a most pleasing, almost cloud-like, display. Against a darker background of shrubs or trees this is an effective plant, and it is easy to grow almost anywhere except where damp. Naturally, it demands space, but it will not take advantage of this since it has no vices — other than leaving a large gap after its three- or four-weeks period in flower.

Crocosmia

For a plant to be in cultivation in Britain for a generation or more without its value being recognised is not, I have discovered, at all unusual. But for such a plant to be shown for the first time at the Royal Horticultural Society's hall in Westminster and to be given both an Award of Merit and a First Class Certificate must be very exceptional. This happened when I submitted *Crocosmia masonorum* in 1963, and the background story to this needs to be recorded.

My first stock came from the Continent in 1953 with a warning that it was not quite hardy. I was most impressed by the flame-orange trumpet flowers on wiry 2-foot stems, which though akin to montbretia in form, were carried on an arching terminal spray so as to face upwards to the sun and to the human eye. Its effect is startling and with fine strap-like ribbed foliage to match, it had all the makings of a first class plant — if only it were fully hardy. For the first two years, with only a few corms, I lifted and dried them off for the winter as with gladiolus. After this I risked leaving some outdoors, but covered the spot with leaves. They came through and flowered much more freely than before, but it was not until 1961 that I had sufficient to risk a few without any protection at all. But when it came to January, 1963, with a thousand or so in the nursery as well as my group in the garden I feared the worst. The soil, having no snow cover, was frozen solid to an average depth of 20 inches, encasing the corms in ice. Scarcely one was lost and the slur that hampered the acceptance of *C. masonorum* as a hardy plant must be wiped out for ever, for as far as I can gather, this was the verdict of others who left it to fend for itself during that grim winter. It needs to be left alone, once planted in the sunny position and light soil it prefers, for at least three or four years. The corms are not large, and in the first year are rather shy to flower. But after that they settle down and if spaced about 6 inches apart when first planted, they will fill out and make a massive clump of incomparable beauty, attractively foliaged before and after the July–August flowering period, when it becomes a splendid sight.

Cynara

There are ornamental species of rhubarb (*Rheum*) and of onion (*Allium*) but apart from chives (*Allium schoenoprasum*) I can think of only one vegetable that is worthy of a place purely on its merits as a decorative plant. This is *Cynara scolymus*, the globe artichoke, and a very handsome subject it is in the mauve-purple form. Apart from its statuesque height of 5 or 6 feet, it is on somewhat similar lines to a relative mentioned earlier (p. 43), *Centaurea pulchra major*. Deeply jagged, wide-spreading greyish leaves hang obliquely from a large woody-rooted plant, and above these a thick, grey, leafy stem towers to carry round heads with a tufted crest of colour in high summer. The edible part is the bud, a tight, green, scaly sphere, and the scales themselves when cooked are considered a delicacy. Not caring for fancy foods which are fiddling to eat, I prefer to see them flower and allay hunger by eating something more substantial.

Cynara is not the hardiest of perennials and is best in deep light soil and full sun. My stock was decimated in the 1963 winter and though such frosts come but seldom, I now take the precaution of covering them with straw or tops.

CHAPTER FIVE

Dicentra to Euphorbia

It is difficult to decide how to treat the delphinium, having reached its alphabetical position, especially as some enthusiasts have awarded it the title of Queen of the Border. Such a title, to my mind, should not be given to any one subject if only because a border worthy of the name should contain a variety of plants. To allow a border to be dominated by, much less to be composed entirely of, one plant, despite variations of colour, is to shut the mind off from all the wealth of beautiful forms existing in other plants. Those who have borders of more or less all one kind of plant are merely backing their own fancies and this may give them greater pleasure. But the title Queen of the Border assumes that the delphinium has superlative qualities over all other plants, and this is simply not true. Every distinct plant has its own beauty, and comparisons between them become out of place, if not odious. Delphiniums have an incomparable beauty, but so have many other plants, and since it is with some of these, which are less well known, that I am most concerned in this book, there is no need for me to include them.

Dicentra

To some extent the same remarks apply to dianthus, including Border Pinks, but when it comes to dicentra the case is greatly altered. The true Bleeding Heart, *Dicentra spectabilis*, is among the choicest of plants but it cannot be said to be a difficult one to grow. It sells each year in its thousands and yet one seldom sees it in gardens, but perhaps this is a case of not taking the trouble to do a little arithmetic. My guess is that possibly 40,000 plants are sold annually by retailers in this country. It sounds a lot, but for the past 12 years over 300,000 new houses have been built each year and if one half these have gardens which the owner cultivates, and if half again are would-be purchasers of a plant of dicentra, it

Eryngiums belong to the thistle family, and *E. alpinum* is most attractive with its ruff of silvery leaves surrounding the blue flower cones

Crocosmia masonorum prefers a light soil and sunny position and, once it has settled down, will make a massive group of brilliant flame coloured flowers

Left: *Euphorbia myrsinites* bursts into flower in the spring with a cluster of greenish-yellow blooms   Right: *Gentiana sino-ornata* has bright blue flowers, with purplish-blue bands on the outside of the petals. It needs a lime-free soil

Ballerina is an apt name for this variety of *Geranium cinereum*; the delicate red veining on the petals runs into a splash of red at the flower centre

still leaves a margin of unsatisfied demand to the tune of 35,000 not counting the backlog of older gardens. Such a calculation, however, leads nowhere, except to emphasise my belief that the majority of gardeners are still unaware of the charms of this beautiful plant. Its roots are rather ugly-looking fangs, spreading out menacingly from a tight central stock in which pinkish shoots are lurking. But it is none the less a fragile plant and both shoots and roots are easily damaged. It resents being divided and indeed often defies division except with a knife, and younger nursery-grown plants are always the best investment. There is a risk of damage, too, from late spring frosts, when the sprays of foliage are unfurling to show the first of the crimson and white lockets dangling along the arching stems. But with care these disabilities can be mitigated if not always avoided. A site should be selected with some shelter of a wall or evergreens which will break the coldest, strongest winds, for though the plant itself is completely hardy, the top growth is susceptible to damage. The soil should be deeply dug and enriched with humus or compost, and the drainage should be good. The plants need a wide planting hole and firming should be done gently, but having done this there is no reason why they should not give good returns for several years, and from late April to mid-June be a source of special joy.

One of the best specimens I ever saw of *D. spectabilis* was in Northern Sweden and there, too, it is known as Bleeding Heart or Dutchman's Breeches. Its third folk name is Lady of the Bath and though one has to turn an individual locket upside down and draw back the twin keels of red, it needs little imagination to see the pistil looking very much like a white lady in her bath.

Dicentra eximia is easy enough to grow in sun or partial shade, with pretty, glaucous green, parsley-type leaves, densely erect to about 10 inches with stumpy sprays of magenta-rose lockets dangling above. The roots are not fangy but make a wide matted clump which, unlike that of *D. spectabilis*, will easily divide in autumn or early spring. The flowering period is spring, but there is a white variation, *D. eximia alba*, which continues flowering on and off all summer in good soil, though this is not a sturdy, reliable grower. *Dicentra eximia* is known in the North Country as Keys of Heaven but I can offer no explanation for this.

A few years ago there came from the United States a hybrid called

4

Bountiful, with flowers a little larger and more richly coloured. This is a good plant, except for the risk of some rot attacking older plants where the soil is damp. This is not very serious for it seems to arise only when growth has been extra luxuriant, and with me sufficient new growth has always appeared the following spring to make good any loss. Other hybrids have since come from America, the deeper red Paramount and the ivory-pink Silversmith, but neither of these seem to be robust. More recently, a seedling from Bountiful appeared at Bressingham and it has been named Adrian Bloom, after my son, for I am old-fashioned enough to like using family names for some outstanding plants raised here, and this dicentra fully qualifies. It is a little taller than Bountiful, larger flowered and deeper coloured, a glowing crimson shade with very attractive foliage. It is about 15 inches high, and, like Bountiful, has a habit of often flowering a second time in early autumn.

Dictamnus
Dictamnus fraxinella, not the annual kochia, is the true Burning Bush. When in flower on still, hot days, it is possible to ignite as a brief flash the volatile gas given off by this plant. It has stiff spikes to $2\frac{1}{2}$ to 3 feet set with lilac or pinkish flowers like rounded butterflies, tapering towards the tip. Spring growth is tardy. The plants are deep-rooted and like to be left alone. With this plant, too, attempted divisions will probably be fatal, but it comes from seed, given patience. It likes full sun and needs little by way of richness and moisture so long as its roots can penetrate deeply. The leaves are dark green and shiny, resembling those of the ash tree — hence the specific name. I am using the older name of *fraxinella* quite deliberately, knowing that *D. albus* is said now to be correct. But this is misleading and confusing because there is also a white variation. *D. fraxinella* is well known and quite pleasing as well as being a descriptive name, with *D. fraxinella alba* applicable to the white form. To use *D. albus* for the pink or lilac and to add *albiflorus* for the white is surely an unnecessary complication.

Dodecatheon
I am trying to keep the range of distinctive plants to those fully hardy and fairly adaptable to different types of soil. It is tempting to include the charming dierama, the Wand Flower, but this grows well

only on lime-free soil that does not dry out. For anyone with such conditions, the pendulous slender stems with their dangling pink flowers in summer are a rare sight, especially if it can be used beside a pool. It is not, however, a bog plant nor are the dodecatheons, those little-grown cousins of the primula. They are woodland plants and where some shade is possible without being parched, they make quite a splash with their reflexed petals of purple and rosy-mauve and orange centres. Shooting Stars is an apt folk name for these, and though there are several species they do not differ enough to name them here. Any seen or offered would fill one's need. They flower in late spring, usually 9 to 15 inches tall, are long lived and are dormant from July to March.

Epimedium

Epimediums, too, are woodlanders, but are adaptable to any but hot, dry positions. It is intriguing to reflect that these are relatives of the berberis, though there is little superficial resemblance. It is also interesting to note how in very recent years the demand has suddenly outstripped the supply as it has with a few other plants, notably hostas and bergenias. This is because gardening folk have woken up to the fact that there is a special value in plants which have good foliage for ground cover as well as having worth while flowers, and can be left to take care of themselves for years without becoming a nuisance.

Epimediums have an appearance of delicacy, especially in spring, which tends to underrate their toughness when it comes to survival. Their spread comes from somewhat woody shoots just below the surface, and though feeding roots are fibrous, the one reason for them being able to hold their own in company with the roots of trees is that the greenery they supply holds very little moisture. The foliage is in fact somewhat papery in texture on stems no more fleshy than a robin's legs. These stems support the foliage like a canopy, and though a new set of leaves is made every year, it is only during early spring, when flowering time comes, that foliage is absent. This is one of the most distinctive features of epimediums and it makes them most attractive. Flowers are in small sprays only a few inches high, starry or spidery of appearance in white, pink, yellow and browny-orange, and in some the fresh apple green tinges of foliage which quickly follow flowering have russet and purple tints as well.

It is scarcely a case here of saying which are the best epimediums to grow, for so much would depend on finding any at all. None need to be spurned, for none are coarse and all are pretty. *Epimedium grandiflorum* (syn. *E. macranthum*) has variations in light and deep pink flowers carried on stems up to 12 inches high followed by leaves of dark green and tinted with bronzy-purple. *E. pinnatum colchicum* is yellow flowered and has leaves of apple green, while the vigorous *E. perralderianum* has flowers of yellow and brown and a wealth of pretty leaves. *E. pinnatum* is also sturdy and has several variations in colour of flower if not in foliage. *E. rubrum* is deep red, shorter than most in leaf and flower, and *E. youngianum* also keeps closer to the ground, with *E. y. niveum* a white-flowered variant and *roseum* a pink. *E. warleyense* is quite charming. Its flowers are a deep orange shade and the very decorative foliage reaches 12 inches.

As with other somewhat neglected genera, names, too, have become a trifle confused, especially as some obscure hybrids have lurked here and there in gardens. The next few years are almost certain to witness a rising popularity of epimediums, for they have great potential in the modern way of gardening. But just because they are adaptable to some of the less hospitable shady places, let it not be thought that they do not respond to kindness. They do. An occasional mulch with peat and added fertiliser, some compost or any sort of humus, will bring good dividends and they will spread much more quickly where a reasonable amount of moisture is not lacking.

Eryngium

By comparison with most flowers the eryngiums are freakish, as if their particular lead in natural evolution went off the rails somewhere. Though quite widely distributed in Nature, all have flowers without visible petals. In some, stems are as brightly coloured as the flower bracts and in others the flowers and leaves alike are green. The latter are natives of the New World and some flower arrangers find them distinctive. Such species as *Eryngium serra*, *E. bromeliifolium* and *E. pandanifolium* grow from large green rosettes of vicious looking saw- or tooth-edged leaves and send up stiffly branching spikes tipped by green spiny thimbles as flowers. One of the prettiest is the true Sea Holly, *E. maritimum*, which name is sometimes applied collectively to the genus. This is, however, a spindly little plant heavily silvered of leaf and faintly blue of flower and really happy only in sandy or seaside gardens. *E. alpinum* is very handsome, with rounded green leaves and sturdy 2- to 2½-foot stems crowned with large, whiskery, silver-blue flowers. Though there are improved forms such as Donard Variety or Amethyst, I find a tendency for all to rot away here and there in winter. A dryish soil and full sun help to keep a group intact and occasionally self-sown seedlings appear.

Eryngium bourgatii, a Pyrenees native, is pretty reliable. This is very silvery with a tinge of blue in the 20-inch stem as well as in the terminal bract. One excellent species with silver-blue stems and flowers is *E. variifolium* and this has the advantage of marbled evergreen foliage. This reaches 2 feet and *E. dichotomum* is also good on somewhat similar lines. *E. giganteum*, growing a good 3 feet is quite imposing, but it is only biennial. *E. oliverianum* and such hybrids as *amethystinum* and Violetta are most attractive with bright blue flowers and upper stems and shiny green dandelion-type leaves. Deep fleshy roots often make new plants even if the crowns occasionally rot away, but bare gaps in a group are not infrequent. *E. planum* is easy, green and leafy but for the blue flowering tips, but these are not so bright as in the widely branching *E. tripartitum* and this to my mind is the best of this group which grows to 3 to 3½ feet. A dwarfish silvery-blue species has recently appeared in *E. leavenworthii*, which promises well and is later to flower than most others which cover the middle weeks of summer.

Eupatorium

Tall subjects with the built-in ability to stand erect are worthy of note because so many lack this quality. In any case, the eupatoriums are not well known and at least two are good garden plants. The first is *Eupatorium rugosum* (syn. *E. fraseri* and *E. ageratoides*) and it makes a stout leafy bush 4 feet high covered in small flattish heads of fluffy white flowers in later summer. It is an easy plant with no vices but for occasional self-sown seedlings, and adaptable for sun or partial shade so long as the soil is not too dry. *E. purpureum* has a wide purple-rose head of flower towering up to a good 7 feet high, on very stiff stems. This is, of course, too tall for small gardens and unless one can view downhill to it the flower head cannot fully be seen. Nevertheless, it is an imposing plant, and in reasonably moist conditions the purple-tinged stem and leaves enhance the picture it makes. Plants grow into quite massive clumps and do not as a rule deteriorate with age, but what I like most about it is that it comes into full glory just when summer is fading into autumn.

Euphorbia

If eryngiums can be described as being a trifle freakish it would be difficult to find a phrase that would cover the euphorbias, a vast genus that includes some definite oddities. Hardy perennial species available for British gardens are, however, more orthodox, but all have bracts or clustered flower heads and the characteristic white sap in the leaves and stems, called 'pigeon's milk' in country districts. *Euphorbia characias* and *E. wulfenii* are so much alike for garden purposes that they can be described together. They are sub-shrubs, with year-round, blue-grey foliage of a succulent nature, and slowly build up into an imposing plant 3 feet high or more till they startlingly burst into almost a fountain of sulphur-yellow heads of flower in spring. These are scarcely plants for an ordinary border, but they look well with shrubs or on a wall. They prefer privation to richness, and though old plants may die and though winters like that of 1963 may reduce them to pulp, there are usually sufficient self-sown seedlings around to refurnish the group, so long as these are transplanted when quite small. Old plants resent being moved.

One of the best of all spring-flowering herbaceous plants is *E. epithymoides* (syn. *E. polychroma*). It is very sturdy and hardy and remains compact. During March, purplish shoots poke through to provide heads of bright sulphur-yellow bracts in April and early May. These reach 18 inches high by the time they begin to fade imperceptibly to green, and by then green leaves are helping to make the neat 20-inch bush of foliage it remains until autumn.

Euphorbia griffithii was introduced from the Himalayas a few years ago. Planted beneath high trees it grew well though the stems were lax and the flower heads a trifle dull. Among some young plants I received in 1953 was one that stood stiffly erect in the open and the flower heads were of a rich burnt orange shade. Tests and trials pointed strongly to this being a variation and on the strength of its apparently improved colour and habit, I named it Fireglow. In fairness it must be said that one or two who have purchased this stock have said they can see no difference. But others agree with my contention that Fireglow is an improvement. Given an open site it is a very good plant, with slow-spreading shoots from below ground that come through at first like asparagus to show the deep fiery heads in May and June. Afterwards these, too, fade into the greenery of a stiff shapely bush, 2½ feet high with no suggestion of stem weakness.

Euphorbia myrsinites and *E. biglandulosa* are rather alike. Both have almost prostrate, silver-blue stems with fleshy leaves carried in Monkey Puzzle formation. In the fullness of time — usually after two years' growth — tips of mature stems burst into flower, a wide posy of pale greenish-primrose, during spring. The plants are cheerful looking throughout the year, but can be damaged by severe winters. Both are best in very well-drained soil.

One of the most neglected euphorbias is *E. palustris*, and it is a British native. It likes moisture, as the name implies, and makes a large plant with very tough roots. Lush and leafy stems run up quickly in spring to 3 feet or more, and by late May or early June the plants are heavy headed with a mass of light sulphur-yellow. It is a plant that needs a fair amount of space and in the right position makes a pleasing display.

The vernal shoots of *E. sikkimensis* are sheathed with leaves of much more vivid colour than the sulphury-yellow flowers that follow many weeks later. Purple-crimson tinged with lighter shades, these shoots are most attractive and by late April reach a foot or so high. Then the stem runs up, clothed in willowy green leaves and at 4 feet or more high the flower heads colour up in July and August. This, too, is a worthy, trouble-free plant, at home in both sun and partial shade.

The biennial or otherwise monocarpic *E. lathyrus*, the Caper Spurge, has become notorious not for its appearance but for its supposed mole-repellent qualities. I have not found time to make my own experiments and unless it can be of proven value against moles will remain a sceptic. I doubt very much any mole-deterrent

properties; at least two people I know have methodically tried it
without any success at all. My little colony of this plant is round a
fine old Scots Pine, the roots of which would deter moles from
working anyway. Every season requests come from our retailing
customers for some client wanting a few seedlings as a result of
reading about its mole-bane qualities, and so the colony of plants
remains a small one. This species has, however, some decorative
merit, growing stiffly as it does with outstretched close-set leaves of
glaucous blue with a whitish midrib and, finally, a head of sulphury
flowers.

CHAPTER SIX

Filipendula to Hosta

A good deal of confusion has followed the division of spiraeas into separate genera. What were once *Spiraea aruncus* (Goat's Beard) and *S. filipendula* (Meadowsweet) have now the specific epithet as the generic name. It might have been worse perhaps, for at least there is a practical outcome, since it appears that the filipendulas are now those with a head of flowers, whereas the aruncus have spikes and this leaves spiraea to cover all the shrubby kinds. I am still a little uncertain, however, on the most up-to-date classification of the filipendulas, but will try to simplify. *Filipendula digitata* seems to cover by its name the dwarfer variations with fingery leaves. These are bright green and very abundant and through them come wide heads of glistening pink flowers. What I know as *F. digitata nana* grows only 6 to 9 inches high, but there is another of 15 to 18 inches and a third of about 2 feet. Height varies with moisture and richness, for though these pretty plants are not difficult, like astilbes they cannot flourish and give a good display unless their basic needs are met. *F. palmata* is on the same lines, but has broader and less divided foliage. The finest variation was known as *F. palmata rubra*, but *F. purpurea* is now said to be correct. This is best in some shade and is more fussy for moisture than most, but it is a very beautiful plant, reaching 2½ feet with heads of brightest carmine-rose. *F. elegantissima* would appear to be closely linked, but this is taller and sturdier, of a clear light pink shade. Then there is *F. gigantea* (syn. *F. camtschatica*), massive in every way, but though the heads are 9 inches across the colour is on the pale side. All are good where moisture is not lacking and none need staking. This, of course, also applies to the true Meadowsweet, *F. ulmaria*, of which there are no very exciting variations. The one exception to this list of moisture lovers is *F. hexapetala*. The double-flowered form, *plena*, is a first-rate plant and is happy in full sun as well as being quite resistant to drought. The leaves are dark green, rather like parsley, and in June and July stiffly branching stems about 20 inches high have fulsome heads of intensely white flowers. The complementary effect of foliage and flower is very pleasing indeed. In rich, moist soil, *F. rubra* (syn. *F. venusta magnifica*) is magnificent. It has wide heads of glistening pink on very strong stems 4 to 5 feet high in June to August, with fingered foliage. Plants grow robustly with a fairly rapid spread in good soil.

Gentiana

The name gentian has become so closely associated with alpine and rock gardens that many people are surprised when they learn that some species grow to 4 feet high. In between the true alpine and these tall and not very special herbaceous species, there are a few first-class garden plants, of which one outstanding example is the willow gentian, *Gentiana asclepiadea*. This carries deep blue trumpets on slender stems about 2 feet high in late summer, but is much better in cool shade than in fully open or dry positions. It dies down in winter to a compact root which dislikes being moved, much less divided. In just the right conditions it will naturalise. Of a similar height or a little taller is the beautiful but somewhat baffling *G. makinoi*, which makes a leafy, fairly erect bush with a startling terminal cluster of rich blue flowers in July and August. I used the adjective 'baffling' because it is so slow to increase. Division is very tricky, and I find seedling plants need coddling for three or four years before they make a show, and although I first saw the species on a fairly dry part of the rock garden at Kew, at Bressingham it is best in deep, moist loam. *G. axillariflora* is said to be on similar lines but easier, but at the time of writing it has only just been planted in my garden.

It is surprising that so little use is made in frontal border groups of the summer-flowering gentians of which *G. septemfida* is best known. Although none exceed 9 to 10 inches in height they make such a wonderful show and are quite happy in ordinary soil, with or without lime. Any of the following kindred species will serve this purpose: *G. bisetaea*, *G. doeringiana*, *G. hascombensis*, *G. lago-dechiana* as well as *G. septemfida*, but there is a specially good variant of the latter in *latifolia*. All have bright blue trumpets clustered on somewhat lax, leafy stems, and all much prefer to be left alone once planted. Attempts to divide them mostly fail, but with care and patience they will come from seed. In lime-free soils, such autumn gentians as *G. sino-ornata* and some of its hybrids can also be used to very good effect as frontal groups.

Geranium

One of the most persistent and lingering misconceptions relating to plants is that of the true nature of geraniums. The fact is that practically all true geraniums are hardy, but large numbers of people still know as geraniums what are in fact pelargoniums, of which only one obscure species — *Pelargonium endlicherianum* — has any suggestion of being a hardy perennial. It would almost seem, judging by the awakening interest in true geraniums that their value as garden plants is only just becoming appreciated. The majority are of the easiest culture and a large proportion are adaptable for both sun and shade. These have a remarkable capacity for not only surviving under harsh and poor conditions but of making a show, even if this falls well short in duration compared to plants with access to more substantial nutriment. For example, *Geranium armenum* (a name preferable to *psilostemon*, now said to be correct) will grow $3\frac{1}{2}$ feet in a dense bush given ample moisture as against barely 2 feet where starved and dry. The flowers, over 1 inch across on wide branching stems, are fiercely magenta from June to August, and because of this adjoining groups need to be chosen with care. I find yellows and light blues or whites cause no clashing.

Geranium endressii is more commonly seen in gardens. Dense mounds of light green, and sprays of light or bright pink make a good show in June and July. The height is 20 to 24 inches and growth is very lush though much subdued when near or under trees. A. T. Johnson, Rose Clair and Wargrave Pink are the best varieties, differing but little. *G. grandiflorum* spreads too quickly for what it gives in flowers, but Johnson's Blue is very good indeed. It smothers itself in early summer in wide, blue, saucer-shaped flowers, and reaches a height of 18 inches. *G. ibericum* is taller at 2 feet or so, dark of leaf and a rich deep blue. It often flops with heavy rain and should be cut hard back after flowering so as to promote a new crop of leaves which in themselves are quite pleasing. *G. macrorrhizum* is not spectacular, having light pink veined flowers for a short period, but the leaves are good ground cover in sun or shade, smelling when crushed of Sweetbriar, and there is a pretty form with variegated foliage.

The common English name of Meadow Cranesbill applies to *G. pratense*, but one would not use this or its white or pink variations unless an extensive collection was required. Having made a collection of seventy or eighty species and varieties of geraniums, I find it a little difficult to cut down severely here, but there are three double-flowered Cranesbills I cannot omit. They rank as old-fashioned plants come to light again and they are good value for modern gardens. The flowers are $1\frac{1}{2}$ inches across, almost fully double, reaching 2 feet in average soil, branching quite widely from a compact, deep-rooted plant and flowering in June and July. The light blue is *G. pratense coeruleum plenum* and the darker violet-blue is *G. p. purpureum plenum*. There is also a double white, *album plenum*, said to be rare, but I find it grows just as easily as the other two.

Geranium renardii is a little charmer, in spite of its having a rather brief period in flower. The flowers are sizeable shallow cups of lightest mauve-blue, marked with intriguingly delicate crimson veins within. These disappear in June under a 10-inch canopy of greyish leaves, downy and stippled and so remaining until autumn. It is easy to grow, best in sun and a plant most people find engenders affection. *G. sanguineum* spreads, but not to become a nuisance. Any excessive exuberance can be forgiven because of the long succession of magenta-rose flowers in the solid twiggy-stemmed mound it makes, only 12 inches high. A good clear pink hybrid exists in Holden Variety and there is a white form, *album*, that is quite pleasing, apart from another good pink known as *lancastriense splendens* which makes a 12-inch mound and keeps flowering for about 10 weeks. The variety *lancastriense* is itself a useful plant, where a ground-hugging habit is not out of place, but all the variations of *G. sanguineum* have a considerable summer spread even though they die back to a dormant root in autumn.

The value of some geraniums lies in their earliness to flower, followed by foliage which does not leave bare patches for the rest of the summer. This fault applies especially to such early subjects as *Anchusa* and *Papaver orientale*, and for me it offsets the bright display they make. *G. sylvaticum* is among those that flower in May and June and although the colour is not startling there is no lack of beauty in the salver-shaped flowers nestling above very pretty canopied foliage of buttercup shape, on 18-inch stalks. *G. sylvaticum* is happy in both open and shady places but sunlight enhances the light blue of the variety Mayflower. There are pale pink and white variations, too.

Deeper blue flowers come for several weeks on the densely spreading mounds of the uncommon but easy *G. wlassovianum*. This covers the July–September period and though one is apt to boggle at the name, the plant itself is worth a place where space is not restricted. With an even wider spread each summer, *G. wallichianum* Buxton's Blue has saucer-shaped flowers nearly 2 inches wide, of both light and dark blue. The effect is very cheerful indeed and though this has been said to be rather tender and best planted in a sheltered shady place, it has proved fully hardy at Bressingham and has also proved to flourish best in full sun.

For frontal groups where heights of only a few inches offer scope for the dwarfer geraniums, the clear pink, tufty growing *G. dalmaticum* is good. So also is the veined pink *G. farreri* and the very delicate *G. cinereum*, especially the variety Ballerina. These, and the crimson-purple *G. c. subcaulescens*, all have a long season in flower and all are of easy growth. Deep and inhospitable shade will not prevent the 2-foot *G. phaeum* from flowering in May and June. It has tough roots and abundant foliage which, like so many of the taller kinds, needs to be cut back after flowering so as to encourage new greenery. The flowers are small and very dark brownish-purple, but of a mauvish shade in *G. phaeum lividum*. These last two sombre but interesting geraniums come under the appropriate common name of the Mourning Widow.

Gypsophila

To shun in this book the majority of well-known plants is unavoidable, but it does not mean that I consider some to be lacking in distinction. The omissions are made solely in order to devote space to worthy, but less well known, kinds. One could not, for example, regard the sight of a mature planting of the ordinary *Gypsophila paniculata* in its airy cloud of tiny white blossoms without appreciating its charm. The double Bristol Fairy is also deservedly popular, though plants are sometimes short lived, especially where the soil is cold or heavy. The pale pink Flamingo is even more fussy, but there are two long-lived varieties worth mentioning. Both are much dwarfer and compact, and for small gardens this is all to the good. *G. p. compacta plena* grows about 20 inches high but a single plant will still make a wide summer spread. The flowers are double and pure white. Pink Star reaches about 15 inches in height, and though the colour is not deep it is a good and reliable plant for a frontal position where some overhanging does not matter. The variety Rosy Veil is also pale pink, but this runs closer to the ground.

Heliopsis

There are so many hardy perennials with a basically 'daisy' formation that claims to distinction do not come easily to mind. Heleniums and helianthus certainly have a place in a well-stocked bed, but only the heliopsis stand in some need of further emphasis. Despite the fact that all are yellow, they have certain merits not shared by others of the sunflower tribe. The roots are reliably perennial but are never aggressive or troublesome, and although these plants respond best to good soil they hold their leaves during the dry weather better than most plants of this type. In open positions, staking is not needed, and the flowering season covers about 8 to 10 weeks from early July onwards. The first improvements to the type, *Heliopsis scabra*, came with the Continental introduction named *incomparabilis*, over thirty years ago. This appealed to me so much, with its many rows of overlapping petals of warm yellow, $2\frac{1}{2}$ inches across, that I submitted it to the Royal Horticultural Society where it gained an Award of Merit. That was in 1933 and since it was only the second Award of Merit certificate on which my name was written, it was something of a thrill for me. This variety is still popular, but I like the newer Golden Plume even better, for this gained an Award of Merit from the R.H.S. in 1963. There are good single-flowered varieties such as *patula* and *gigantea*, which usually attain $4\frac{1}{2}$ feet against the average of 3 to $3\frac{1}{2}$ feet in other varieties. *H.* Goldgreenheart has a very pleasing greenish suffusion and is aptly named. These five varieties are ample to cover the limited range available unless some real break comes along, and though such varieties as Ballet Dancer, Goldball, Light of Loddon and Zinnia as well as *zinniiflora* are sometimes offered, they are in my experience somewhat superfluous.

Helleborus

Helleborus niger, the Christmas Rose of evergreen appeal, is scarcely a subject for inclusion either in a bed of assorted perennials or in this book. But *H. orientalis* is, even though many people would prefer to see it among shrubs or in some special place. This is the Lenten Rose and is much more adaptable than *H. niger*. Given some shade for preference and good deep soil, it can be a source of joy in February and March long before other plants have come to life again. Plants to name or ordered to a specific shade, especially the pinkish or purplish shades, are expensive to buy, but these usually occur in seed-raised plants obtainable from reliable nurserymen. Differing a little in the time at which the annual change of leaf is made, *H. atrorubens* is otherwise near *H. orientalis* in growth, with purplish-crimson flowers during the late winter months before new leaves appear. This is a choice plant which, with me, never sets seed, but I find it well worth the little fussing it needs to ensure a maintained fertility. It is worth noting that all these hellebores make a canopy of leaves if they can, in order to keep the sun from parching the soil below in which their roots are active. A spring mulch helps them to do this, and makes for strong, healthy and attractive growth.

Helleborus corsicus lacks tidiness and is sometimes damaged by severe frost, but even if complete annihilation occurs as it did widely in 1963, this is a plant one does not like to be without, once having grown it. Light green, leathery leaves grow from not very erect ascending stems till, when mature, a truss of pale apple green flowers appear in early spring. This is charming, and the effect lasts for several weeks. Though best sited in some shade, plants are fairly resistant to drought in spite of them not being deep rooted. I would not down-point *H. corsicus* because of stem weakness for, as a group, stems and foliage merge into loose bush formation up to 2 feet high. For the connoisseur there are a few other helleborus of decided interest, including *H. lividus*, *H. viridis* and the newer *H. sternii*.

Hemerocallis

Hemerocallis, the Day Lily, has a special distinction which is certainly not on the score of rarity, when one considers the vast surge of new varieties it has produced in recent years. This surge is largely due to American hybridists of amateur status whose enthusiasm has been so keen that literally hundreds of new varieties have appeared. As with the iris-minded Americans, the influx of new varieties has brought problems to European gardeners and nurserymen who, in aiming to add the best introductions, have no other means of achieving this than by acquiring far more than can possibly be used. European specialists import new varieties annually, apparently without the slightest co-ordination, with the result that there is nearly as much confusion over here as in the United States. For this reason, any recommendations as to varieties can only be based on those I know and have grown, and readers can be assured that others are in cultivation with equal claims to excellence.

The genus as a whole has strong claims to garden worthiness. The plants grow robustly without being invasive, they have a fairly long flowering season, and are not pernickety about soil, shade or sun. They do, however, respond to good treatment by giving a better, longer display of their richly-coloured trumpet flowers. The breeders have, of course, given us a much wider range of colour than existed in the species, including a reasonably good pink, as in Pink Damask, through every shade of yellow, orange and brown to ruby-mahogany shades like Black Magic. Some of the latter, sometimes described as crimson, maroon or purple and red, fall short of what one would expect and are to my mind rather dull, but where hemerocallis score is in the purer shades of yellow and orange. Hyperion, though older, is still a beauty, and so is the golden-yellow Doubloon. Primrose Mascotte is one of the best light yellows, and Stafford, ruby red; Felicity, ruffled yellow; Golden Orchid; Salmon Sheen, salmon-pink; Pirate's Treasure, salmon-red, flushed vermilion; Larksong, lemon; and Morocco Red are all excellent.

Among the species I have gathered together as garden groups, I like the early-flowering *H. middendorffii*, yellow, and the deeper, long flowering *H. multiflora*, as well as the little *H. minor* which grows only about 12 inches high. These and other species have no doubt been used as parents for the newer named varieties, but should not be despised as being inferior. I know of no hemerocallis without some claim to garden worthiness and it must be a case of individual choice with space limitations in mind. Most varieties are

Left: *Helleborus orientalis*, the Lenten Rose, prefers some shade in which to unfold its pinkish or purplish flowers in March
Right: *Hemerocallis* Larksong is one of the modern hybrid day lilies, lemon-yellow in colour

The compact evergreen leaves and feathery salmon-pink flowers on graceful 18-inch stems make *Heuchera* Splendour a most useful and attractive plant all the year round

Above: *Hosta ventricosa* is an outstanding foliage plant

Left: *Hosta crispula* is one of the most handsome of the hostas; above its creamy-white-edged leaves rise spires of pale lilac flowers

capable of growing into very large plants, three or four of which, after four or five years' growth, would fill the average garden wheelbarrow.

Heuchera

I wish it were possible to make the same remarks about heucheras being everywhere as easy and reliable as hemerocallis. The fact is that on almost any light soil, heucheras grow very well indeed, but they tend to sulk where clay, marl, or wet or very acid conditions prevail. Perhaps I may be excused for saying rather a lot about plants which are not fully adaptable, the reason being that I have been responsible for breeding and introducing most of the modern varieties. In the four localities of East Anglia I have known intimately heucheras have flourished. My father, realising their potentialities for the cut-flower market, began breeding as long ago as 1920, and since 1930 I have carried on. The first break (and the first award from the Royal Horticultural Society) came in 1932 when Bloom's Variety showed that greater freedom in flower of one parent had been married with richness in colour of the other. Older varieties had one or the other but not both together. Heucheras have that all too rare combination of compact, well-foliaged evergreen growth and a show of brightly coloured flowers carried daintily on sprays or spikes for several weeks in early summer. Some have very pretty leaves, shaped much like the geranium, in varying shades of green, sometimes with darker zonings for good measure. The stems are thin and wiry, varying from 15 to 30 inches high, and the number of individual flowers, small and bell-shaped, on a well grown plant, run into hundreds. Colours range from white to every shade of pink, through to scarlet and red including coral, salmon and coppery-crimson.

In the course of growing so many for so long, I have learned that heucheras must firstly have good drainage, and are best in sun or only partial shade. They flower better for being enriched, yet they are drought resistant. Their two faults must not be overlooked because of my partiality. The first is susceptibility to late spring frosts which may spoil the first flush of unfurling sprays. The second fault is that the crowns become woody with age, and the remedy, often needed every three or four years, is to mulch deeply

with soil or compost, or to dig up and replant deeply, using only
the most vigorous shoots and discarding older woody growth.

My selection of the best varieties is Carmen, intense pink, 2
feet; Firebird, bright red, 2 feet; Freedom, rose-pink, 1½ feet;
Bloom's Variety, coral-red, 2 feet; Ibis, clear pink; Bressingham
Blaze, salmon-red, 20 inches; Scintillation, bright pink, tipped
coral, 2 feet; Sparkler, carmine and scarlet, 2 feet; Splendour,
salmon-scarlet, 2 feet; and Red Spangles, 20 inches. And in the less
expensive Bressingham Hybrids, one may expect many shades
representative of the infinite range these beautiful plants possess.

Heucherella

In the process of breeding heucheras at Bressingham came a cross
between a selected hybrid and one of its cousins, the *Tiarella*
species named *wherryi*. This has golden-green speckled leaves and
feathery sprays of creamy-white flowers only 12 inches high. One
seedling only came from the cross and proved to have acquired good
points from both the parents — a very long flowering season, neat
habit, good foliage but with larger and more colourful flowers than
the *Tiarella* parent. According to the rules, this bigeneric hybrid
or 'mule cross' had to be given a name to show its mixed marriage
origin and is now known as *Heucherella* Bridget Bloom. It is a
splendid little plant for fairly good light soil, preferring a little
shade, and in moist seasons has been known to flower almost as
freely in autumn as at its normal period of May and June, with a
profusion of light pink sprays 15 inches high.

Hosta

In spite of my complaint that several worthy plants are still suffering from neglect, there is one genus which has come into its own
in recent years in no uncertain manner. It is the hosta, formerly
known as funkia. Thirty years ago only a few nursery catalogues
listed just a few kinds; nowadays the difficulty is for nurserymen to
hold on to sufficient stocks to list. Much has been written about
their virtues and this has stimulated a demand which is not likely
to be fully met for years. They are certainly plants of distinction.
As could be expected, these plants which have aroused interest after
long neglect and among which are hybrids of obscure origin,
have a somewhat confused nomenclature and this has not yet

finally been cleared up because of disagreement between authorities who have worked upon the genus.

Hostas possess practically all the good points needed for first-class garden plants: hardiness, adaptability, reliable growth and good foliage, coupled with pleasing overall appearance. They have no real fads other than a dislike of parched conditions, and they will grow in shade or sun so long as their roots can find moisture and nutriment. Once settled they can be left for years to develop gradually as solid clumps. Ideally, all like a fair amount of moisture and most are definitely happiest in cool shade. They vary in height from 8 inches to 4 feet and so can be used in a wide range of places from waterside to woodland conditions, for edging and for a mixed bed or border. Spacing is important. With such plants foliage counts at least as much as the flowers and the larger-growing kinds need room in which to develop individually. All lose their leaves at the onset of winter.

Glaucous-leaved kinds include *Hosta fortunei* which is in fairly good supply. This flowers in June, with smooth stems to about 2 feet set with mauve-blue flowers. The leaves are abundant, 12 to 15 inches long and pointed, and there is a larger form in *H. fortunei robusta*. *H. lancifolia* has narrower laurel-green leaves, ribbed and pointed as the name indicates. These overlap to good effect, and flowers of a lavender shade on 18-inch stems come in August. There is a larger form named *H. l. fortis*, and one of the same general appearance but very much smaller and later flowering named *tardiflora*. It is scarcely necessary to describe all the green-leaved hostas. I know of none unworthy of a place where space exists, but of the rest, *H. ventricosa* is outstanding, with fine large leaves and 3-foot spikes of violet-mauve in July and August. Then there is the bluish grey-green *H. sieboldiana*. This has leaves more rounded and prominently ribbed, and the flowers are pale lilac-mauve, 2 feet or so in the type and 3 feet in the form *elegans*. Light lettuce-green is the foliage shade of *H. plantaginea*, a late white-flowered species especially partial to moisture and ample humus. Plants need to be well established to flower and though shy flowering is a fault, the clustered trumpets on 2-foot stems are delicately scented. Finally, I should mention one rarity, at present grown under the name *H. rectifolia*. This is quite a giant, running stiffly up to 4 feet, well clothed in leaves which clasp much of the spike as well. The drooping trumpets are violet-mauve, and appear in August and September. Eventually, no doubt, this species will become more plentiful.

Variegated hostas have the greatest appeal. *H. fortunei albopicta* is the finest of these with buff or golden flushed leaves occurring only in spring and early summer. But there are several with long-lasting colourings. *H. undulata medio-variegata* has smallish wavy-edged leaves, growing very compactly with spikes of pale lavender only 18 inches high. This is a delightful little plant and so is *H. albomarginata* with lance-shaped leaves edged with creamy-white variegation. The old variety Thomas Hogg also answers to this description and so in a general way does *H. crispula*, with a crinkly creamy-white edge to the handsome leaves.

When *H. ventricosa aureo-variegata* becomes more plentiful, it is certain to be snapped up quickly whenever seen. It has all the good points of the type, together with the addition of a prominent variegation, well contrasted with the deep green leaves. Some variegated hostas are best ordered when seen in summer for later despatch. Names are not so uniformly accepted as to avoid risk of disappointment, though a nurseryman should not be blamed too harshly if he errs in spite of honest attempts to be correct.

The present scarcity is, however, tempting some nurserymen to raise hostas from seed. It is a slow process and takes three to four years for plants to reach a good size for flowering. Such seedlings are likely to show variations and may even yield some valuable new forms in due course. For many gardeners, seedlings, so long as they are offered as such, will fill a need for less expensive plants, but because increase by division is rather slow, the best species and forms true to name are likely to be somewhat expensive. But there, hostas are plants of real distinction and have all the attributes of a good investment.

CHAPTER SEVEN

Incarvillea to Lysimachia

Flowers of an exotic appearance are rarely seen among hardy perennials, although this adjective has rather an artificial connotation. If it can be applied to something more likely to be seen in tropical conditions, then it is safe to use it for the incarvilleas, with flowers showing considerable resemblance to the big 3-inch trumpets of the gloxinias. They grow from thick fleshy roots, like fingers and thumbs joined at the top which are very tardy in sending up new shoots in spring. But from dormancy in April, they are usually in flower before May is out. The two species usually available are *Incarvillea delavayi* and *I. grandiflora*. The former runs up as it flowers to about 2 feet by the time it has finished, displaying quite prominent seed-pods. Leaves follow the stems, but for all the fragile appearance of the reddish-pink trumpets they are seldom spoiled by rough weather. The variety Bees' Pink is a pleasing shade of rose-pink and does not grow quite so tall. The leaves are long, deeply cut and dark green, as with *I. grandiflora*, but this is a much dwarfer plant with bright, deep rose trumpets disproportionately large. Incarvilleas like sun and well-drained soil and *I. grandiflora* especially needs to be placed where it will not be overhung. They do not lend themselves to division, but seedlings, though slow to grow and fiddling to handle, are the best means of increase.

Jurinea
Jurinea is a generic name scarcely ever seen. It covers a small range of perennials related to centaurea or Knapweed and I find one of them, *Jurinea glycacantha*, well worth a place. It forms a neat bush 3 feet high of dark green leaves, prettily divided, and the branching stems carry a wealth of purple tufts from late June to early August. It is a very accommodating plant with no fads other than a liking for a place in the sun, and though it could not be regarded as spectacular, I like it.

Kirengeshoma

Kirengeshoma palmata is a native of Japan. It has waxy looking flowers like small day lilies of soft yellow for many weeks of later summer, nodding over a mass of light greenery. The leaves are saw-edged and of nettle type but the whole plant has a distinctive appearance, at once bushy and graceful, reaching 3 feet high where moist. It is, however, not by any means a bog plant. What it likes is a humus-rich soil, some high shade and no lack of moisture, and though it makes no brilliant display, it is the type of plant one feels glad to have. It is not difficult and makes a stout clumpy plant which can be divided with care. A fault is a liability to be damaged by late spring frosts, just as the leaves are unfurling.

Kniphofia

I cannot help having wistful thoughts upon kniphofias. As a producer of hardy plants, these popular Red Hot Pokers are of course always in demand, but over the years I am pretty certain they have been among the least remunerative of nursery stocks I have grown, because they are not all reliably hardy. I am thinking of species and named varieties here because plants raised from seed are much cheaper to grow and of less value because they are always in mixed colours. My experience of the choicer kinds has been a case of working up stocks from division over a period of years only to lose vast numbers when every few years a severe winter has come. One tends to become complacent and drop precautions against frost and snow such as tying up the leaves in November. This would not have helped much in 1963, especially with choice species like *Kniphofia galpinii*, which has thin grassy foliage. My stock of this was well over 2,000 plants in 1962 after a five-year build-up during which none were sold. By the summer of 1963 less than a hundred had survived with which to begin again, and with two or three kinds in smaller quantities the loss was complete.

As natives of South Africa, kniphofias revel in sun and dislike intensely the damp cold of English winters, much less to be in wet soil liable to freeze deeply with little or no snow cover as is so often the case in East Anglia. Among the lessons learned so hardly in 1963 is that older plants of kniphofia are less likely to suffer than young ones, and that perfect drainage is vital. Those growing in my garden suffered least where wet soil had not been trodden on in autumn and where far-ranging tree roots had kept the soil more open. Even so, covering the ground between the plants with straw from November to March, as I have in subsequent winters, must now be a regular practice, though this is not necessary with all kinds of kniphofias in all soils and districts. Such protection — using straw, bracken or similar litter — is a safeguard in cold soils and cold districts for those who have paid good money for choicer species and varieties. Apart from this, kniphofias are trouble-free plants, seldom failing to flower reliably and erectly, and they have overall shapeliness with complementary foliage. They are best used where they can tower above lower-growing plants, or serve as focal points in a mixed perennial bed or border. They should never be overhung. They can, if placed discreetly, break up any tendency to flatness or regularity in a bed or border and are especially effect-ive in groups between or in front of shrubs and evergreens. Few plants can compare with kniphofias for brilliance in shades of yellow, red, flame and orange, and those that flower in autumn are a cheering sight.

Not many true species are widely cultivated and with a good range of named varieties originating from species there is no need to mention more than a few. *K. caulescens* makes a huge clump of wide glaucous bluish leaves and occasionally sends up a heavy spike of flowers which change from dull reddish-salmon to almost white in late summer. This is a plant for isolation rather than among other border plants, as is the earlier flowering *K. tuckii* which has yellow, red-tipped flowers on 4-foot stems. Of the dwarfer species, *K. galpinii* has an exquisite charm. All summer, it has deep green grassy foliage which droops over at the tips, about 15 inches high with no hint of flowers to come till summer is nearly over. Then, in September, the spikes burst through and all through October and often into November there is a fine show of flame-orange pokers, 2 feet high, that are a joy to behold. *K. rufa* is on similar lines but the flowers are yellow, tipped red at first. I do not find this as hardy as *K. galpinii*. *K. macowanii* is grassy leaved and autumn flowering, growing stiffly to 2½ feet with pokers of rich scarlet-flame shade. This is a very good plant not often seen.

Going back in flowering time *K. nelsonii* is also a brilliant flame-red, slightly more broad leaved and at its best in September, with a long period of display. *K. tubergenii* is probably a hybrid to which a Latin name has been given. This makes a shapely, erect, rushy sheaf of bright green leaves nearly 2 feet tall through which rise in June and July pretty spikes of primrose-lemon flowers. Creamy-white, with a flush of pink, is seen in the rare species *K. modesta*. This grows compactly with leaves in more of a rosette formation and closer to the ground than the other species, and the 2-foot flower spikes come in July and August.

One of the earliest hybrids to flower comes from *K. praecox* and it is called Buttercup. This makes its display in late May and June and is followed by the rich orange of Bees' Sunset and the red-tipped, light yellow Springtime. These are all about 3 feet tall. Bees' Lemon is a pleasing shade of yellow, as is the dwarf Gold Else with a long flowering season and bright green slender leaves. The creamy-white Maid of Orleans is exceptionally long flowering, reaching $3\frac{1}{2}$ feet in height and always holding a special appeal. Other summer-flowering yellows include Goldmine and Yellow Hammer; then there is the orange-shaded Ada, and good scarlet and flame shades exist in Alcazar and Underway. The old but reliable Royal Standard is yellow with red tips to the flowers. For a truly majestic, late-flowering, orange-flame variety it would be hard to better Samuel's Sensation.

Though mixed seedlings or hybrids are much less expensive to buy it is the massing of one colour as a group that makes the most telling effect with kniphofias. But whatever the selection, a sunny place and deep light soil well prepared are essential, and a spade is needed for planting. When replanting, it is better to wait until new growth has begun in spring, though summer-flowering kinds can be safely moved after flowering so long as one is prepared to use water if the soil is dry. The old method of tying up the leaves in a bunch to prevent damage by snow or freezing in the crowns is good practice whether or not protective litter is used around the plants to lessen frost penetration in the soil.

Lavatera

There need be no criteria other than that of adaptability or suit-ability as to what should be grown in a mixed flower bed or border. Since I am writing about perennials I would naturally exclude annuals or bedding plants on the score of suitability. But I would not hesitate to use certain shrubs if they fitted in happily, though, generally speaking, this could only apply where they are the better for being cut back every year. Buddleias, for example, should be heavily pruned each spring, but they would still make excessive growth in small or average sized beds. *Lavatera olbia rosea* is pretty robust and is of shrubby growth, yet in most gardens there is a place for it, whether or not it is used among the more usual herbaceous perennials. This is the Tree Mallow and it has one of the longest flowering periods of any plant. It likes a sunny, dry position and will thrive in the poorest and stoniest of soils, branching out from a woody base with stems up to 5 or 6 feet high, decked with pink, salver-shaped flowers about $2\frac{1}{2}$ inches across from early June until the autumn frosts arrive. The leaves are softly grey-green and make a handsome and always colourful show. If need be it can be used as a kind of hedge or a screen to some unsightly object. It has the one fault of exhausting itself after about three years. The drier or poorer the soil, the longer it will live simply because these conditions are more natural for it than richness or moisture, but cuttings or seedlings for replenishment are not difficult to come by.

Liatris

Liatris, or Gay-feathers, have become more widely grown in recent years and their poker spikes, alight with intense lilac inflorescences, are nothing if not striking. These come from a rounded tuber with a flat top which in spring sends out tufts of narrow, dark green leaves and then in June runs up stiff leafy spikes. What makes this unlikely looking member of the daisy family especially interesting is the way in which the flowers begin to open at the top of the spike, instead of at the base, as in practically all other spiky plants. This in itself is a good point, and the overall appearance is marred hardly at all by fading until the flowering stage is over. This covers several weeks from June until well into August and the flowering period can be extended by cutting back in good time — very convenient for those who tend to raid the border for cut flower material! The species of liatris usually offered is *L. spicata* or one of its variants. I find *L. callilepis* the most reliable, with erect spikes up to 3 feet high, and a good dwarf variety exists in Kobold. *L. pycnostachya* is apt to be floppy, but *L. graminifolia* has narrower spikes and a graceful appearance. All liatris

like sun and good drainage, but are otherwise of very easy
culture.

Ligularia

The ligularias have been detached as a separate genus from *Senecio*,
but no one seems to have made it a clear-cut operation so that we
know just which belongs to which. At any rate there is no doubt
about *Ligularia clivorum* and its varieties, which are those with big
handsome leaves above which tower clustered spikes of bright
yellow and orange daisy flowers. These are not plants for dry, over-
crowded borders nor for smaller beds, for they like moisture and
need space in which to show both flower and foliage. Nevertheless,
they are sturdy growing and only in drought conditions do they
suffer. Ideally, single plants need about 3 or 4 square feet in which
to expand to give of their best, preferring sun but not objecting to a
little shade, nor do they mind being in heavy clay. The most dwarf
is the 3-foot *L. clivorum* Gregynog Gold with a mass of deep yellow
flowers in July and August, and the tallest is *L. hessei* — a cross
between *L. clivorum* and *L. wilsoniana* — at 5 to 6 feet. In between
stands Othello with orange flowers and purplish-tinged leaves,
large and handsome. But the finest of all is Desdemona, whose
leaves are of a more decidedly plum-purple hue, with flowers a rich
orange.

Ligularia hodgsonii is dainty by comparison with the *clivorum*
varieties, yet it has the same general appearance, if only a third of
the height at barely 2 feet, when its deep orange-yellow-rayed
flowers are at their best in June. Its leaves are more erect, umbrella-
wise and only 6 to 8 inches across, of smoky purple-green hue.
What was *Senecio przewalskii* has, I believe, been switched to
Ligularia and is one of the most striking of plants for moist soil.
In drier conditions it will survive from year to year but hot or
windy summer days make it flag and droop rather pitifully. Its
leaves are deeply divided and cover the lower parts of the spike as
well, but above, the erect stems are almost black in striking contrast with the bright yellow flowers which taper along the spike to
the tip 6 feet high, at its best in July. Having come across a
variant of this species from a source I omitted to record I tried to
get it identified by a botanical authority. The research failed, for
there was apparently no known variation of *L. przewalskii* and this

brought the recommendation to give it a cultivar name. Hence, The Rocket, which in my estimation is the better of the two. The leaves are less divided and less prone to taking on a ragged appearance, and though the spike and flowers are much the same the overall appearance is more stately and effective.

There are several other ligularias (one should also look under senecio in catalogues) suitable for similar places to those recommended above. Yellow-flowered, on upstanding spikes, lush of foliage and stout of growth, there is the 6-foot *L. macrophylla*, the 5-foot *L. stenocephala* and *L. wilsoniana*. *L. veitchiana* is shorter at 4 feet or so and there is a white-flowered species in *L. smithii*. All are reliably perennial and worthy of inclusion in a garden where there is no lack of moisture and space in which to grow them.

Linum

Blue is the colour usually associated with linum or Flax. Yet in many species, yellow, bright and clear, is seen. Blue or yellow, the Flaxes are sun lovers and are better in dry soils. The blue *Linum perenne* is not very perennial, seldom living beyond two summers and this applies to its other, prettier relatives, *L. austriacum* and *L. tenuifolium*, though self-sown seedlings may make up for losses. *L. narbonnense* is much longer lived, so long as the soil is very well drained, and where happy it is one of the finest of dwarf border plants. The flowers are richly blue and shilling sized and are borne on narrow-leaved bushes about 20 inches high. It makes a brilliant show for ten weeks or more from June to September. Variants with only slight differences are *L. n. gentianoides* and Six Hills.

The yellow linums are perhaps not quite so fussy about sun and drainage, but strongly prefer plenty of both. I have tried several species as frontal groups and find highest marks go to *L. dolomiticum*. This makes a compact root and sends up erect stems to about 18 inches crowned with a wide cluster of brightest yellow rounded flowers ¾ inch across from mid June to late August. The leaves are small but abundant and the whole plant imparts an air of warmth and well-being. *L. campanulatum* is on similar lines, as is *L. flavum*, but I find the latter more leafy and less able to come through wet, cold winters without dying back here and there. This is green-leaved, but *L. paniculatum* is greyish and inclined to be shrubby. The foliage is largely retained during winter and in a warm, sunny spot the plant makes a wonderful show of glistening yellow for many weeks, only 9 inches high. But for suffering from exhaustion after three to four years this would be a first-rate plant, and it is perhaps more often suited to a rock garden or wall top.

Liriope

The name liriope can be found in very few catalogues even where perennials are a speciality, and I fancy several years will elapse before stocks in this country are equal to the demand. This estimation is based mainly on the interest shown by visitors to Bressingham. When I first acquired a few species, my information was that they preferred shade, but in such conditions I found them to be shy to flower. An illustration I saw of a Texas garden where liriope was used to edge a path and made a mass of close-set 9-inch spikes, quickly led me to move mine into full sun, and this is without doubt the position they like best, regardless of the type of soil. My soil is neutral but I doubt if they mind whether the pH is low or high, for they have every appearance of being tough and reliable.

The liriope in the Texas garden was named Majestic, and this a Texas nurseryman subsequently sent me as a gift. It is probably a variety of *L. spicata*, and forms in time a hefty tuft of bright evergreen foliage like a broad-leaved grass arching over towards the ground, from about 8 inches high. Above this come the little poker spikes of a lilac-mauve shade in late summer, but over here it is obviously less free and took months to recover from the 1963 winter. In a more sheltered garden or at the foot of a south-facing wall, I quite think Majestic would be a very good plant both for flowering and ground cover foliage, but I find *L. muscari* fills that dual purpose admirably without finding a special place for it. On my present experience of it, I would award it full marks. The leaves are dark green, and the stiff little spikes of close-set, lilac-mauve heads last for weeks in late summer and autumn with scarcely a hint of fading.

Liriope roots are matted and fibrous and are supplied with small storage tubers which contribute to their drought-resistant greenery. They like being left alone and though the clumps steadily expand, growth is rather slow after being divided. *L. spicata* itself suffered badly in the 1963 winter, though prior to this it flowered freely and regularly on the same lines as *L. muscari* with the colour closer to blue.

The hardiness of some liriopes is in doubt, but *L. muscari* is proven in this respect and is a first-class garden plant which is in the category of 'choice' because it is scarce.

Lychnis

There is much less of the choiceness or scarcity in the *Lychnis* but it is a genus in which colours are truly brilliant. It is a great pity that *Lychnis arkwrightii* is of weak growth, for the colour — as well as the shape — of its flowers is matched only by the brightest of such orange-scarlet phlox as Brigadier and Prince of Orange. It is not a long-lived plant — three or four years at most — and the 9-inch stems are rather lax. Nevertheless, a group planted 6 inches apart gives a bright display during July and August, as does the slightly taller scarlet *L. haageana*, of similar habit. *L. chalcedonica* is much longer lived and much taller. Light green leafy spikes run to 3 feet in good soil, topped by clusters of small, intensely scarlet-red flowers in a head 3 or 4 inches across in June and July. This is the best known of the species of lychnis and one often sees the grey-leaved clumpy *L. coronaria* with its branching spikes of vivid magenta-rose flowers. This, too, is short lived, but self-sown seedlings are mostly to hand. *L. flos-jovis* is much more compact and longer lived. The stems are 9 inches long and erect, from tufty silvery plants, and the bright pink flowers appear in June and July. Then there is the green and leafy *L. dioica* in varying shades. This is as leafy as cabbage lettuce and loosely branching stems reach 18 inches or so. Double-flowered varieties make the best show, and of these Emneth is deep pink and Red Admiral an even deeper shade, almost a red. For sheer intensity, the double cerise-pink flowers of *L. viscaria splendens flore-pleno* would be hard to match. These come on erect 9-inch stems, sticky to the touch, and showing kinship to their relations, the garden pinks. The plants make grassy tufts, spreading a little and needing dividing and replanting every two to three years for good growth. This is a very good plant for June flowering and can be used as an edging.

Lysimachia

The native Yellow Loosestrife is *Lysimachia vulgaris* and quite a good plant for a damp place where it can romp, as it will. *L. punctata* is on similar lines, robust and leafy, with upright pyramidal spikes of bright yellow, sixpenny-sized flowers for many weeks. These are not plants for placing near others that are choice or slow growing, but one could use two white-flowered species more safely. One of these is *L. ephemerum*. It is not everywhere reliable and seems to prefer moist lime-free soil, but the 4-foot tapering spikes and abundant glaucous foliage are most attractive in July and August. *L. clethroides* spreads with moderation, sending up a generous number of 3-foot stems to form a dense erect bush. In late summer, each stem bends over at the tip to send out a curving horizontal spike, up to 6 inches long, of tiny white flowers rather like a buddleia in form. This is a distinctive yet easy growing and adaptable plant which asks for nothing more than ordinary soil which does not parch, and it is useful for cutting.

CHAPTER EIGHT

Macleaya to Origanum

The pleasures that come from building up a collection of plants do not only result from the knowledge one gains of their behaviour. As the collection increases other titbits of knowledge are sure to come your way, for in studying plants and in talking with other plant-lovers one may well find, for example, that errors in identification have sometimes been made. The realm of plants is so immense that no one, however knowledgeable, is error proof and it can be both amusing and instructive to listen to the disputation of experts. Occasionally it may happen that a plant becomes the subject of an argument on the score of identification and leads to research into the sources of nomenclature. Quite a large number have been given their correct names by this means, and to the plant-lover this can be quite exciting if he or she grows the plant in question.

This happened to me in the case of a macleaya (formerly known as bocconia) which I obtained from a college garden in Cambridge where apparently it had been scarcely noticed for years. I was struck by the size of its flowers, for those of the species I had were microscopic in comparison. Two years later I pointed it out to a botanist visiting my garden and he agreed with me that it was quite outstanding with its little pearly flowers on strong and handsomely-leaved 5-foot spikes. As a result of his interest he was able to tell me a month later, after lengthy research, that this was the true *Macleaya cordata* and that what had for a long time been commonly grown under that name was the very different *M. microcarpa*. This itself is a very pretty plant with branching stems rising to 6 feet or more and flowers so numerous as to be almost a haze of brownish-coral in later summer, making it an excellent background plant. But the true *cordata* is more imposing and with its flowers more decided in shape and shade, it merits a position where it can be seen and appreciated. And it is good for cutting.

Macleayas have creeping fleshy roots liable to send up stems after a year or two, beyond their group boundary, but these are not difficult to confine. They grow well in sun or partial shade and flourish in any well-drained soil. The variety Coral Plume is often offered. This is scarcely different to *M. microcarpa* and anyone wishing to have the newly-named, ivory-flowered *M. cordata* should specify with the word 'true' owing to the time lag before the change becomes universally accepted.

Malva

A close relative of *Lavatera olbia rosea* (discussed on p. 73) is *Malva alcea fastigiata*. This plant has much the same satiny pink, mallow flowers as the lavatera but is not shrubby like the latter; the spikes are erect, up to 4 feet high, and it forms a shapely plant which makes a fine display from late July until well into September. This is a plant that should be more widely grown and is specially happy where the soil is dry and rather poor. In winter the whole plant dies back to a woody rooted plant rather like another better known relative, the sidalcea.

Mertensia

It is tempting to include meconopsis, but though this genus embraces some very distinctive plants, most of them have been well written up. In keeping with the intent of this book, the mertensias ought certainly to be included though they are not for gardens where no shade exists. All are blue and all flower in spring, yet apart from having the small tubular form of floret, they vary considerably in growth. *Mertensia ciliata* comes through in spring from fleshy black roots with shoots of smooth glaucous green foliage of broadly tongue shape, branching out and up to about 2 feet. During May and June dangle dozens of little, narrow, bell-shaped flowers of a sky-blue shade. This is a species that does not mind a fair amount of sun so long as the soil is reasonably cool. Another, a little taller, named *M. paniculata* is on similar lines, but the flowers are smaller, and though pretty, it is the less desirable of the two.

The most entrancing of the fleshy-rooted mertensias is *M. virginica*, and in spite of its fault of leaving no surface growth from July to February, there is ample compensation in its spring beauty.

Right: A plant native to Japan, *Kirenge-shoma palmata* prefers a humus-rich soil, and some light shade for producing its waxy yellow flowers

Below: Springtime is a bicoloured kniphofia with large orange and yellow pokers

Left: The intense lilac flowers of *Liatris callilepis* open from the top of the spike downwards instead of from the base, as is common with most spiky plants

Above: *Liriope muscari* is aptly named after the Grape Hyacinth, with its small, round, lilac-blue flowers clustered thickly together in spikes

Left: *Ligularia przewalskii* The Rocket grows to about 6 feet, and has yellow spikes of flowers on black stems

It appears with purplish shoots above ground at crocus time, and in April these change to bluish-green, unfurling and arching to display the near translucent blue trumpets dangling in little clusters along the 2-foot stems. It is a plant of surpassing beauty for several weeks and then with summer's approach it fades away to leave nothing but the black roots below ground. This long resting period is sometimes fatal, not through any inherent weakness but through lack of care on the part of someone out to kill summer weeds, who may be unaware that beneath the soil is a choice and beautiful plant. For this reason and to avoid a gap in a mixed border, it may be safer to use mertensia in some partially shady spot where perhaps daffodils are also grown, for its season of growth coincides with theirs.

Mertensia echioides and *M. primuloides* I have at last concluded are one and the same. This conclusion has been reached as a result of argument over many years with a Dutch acquaintance. At any rate I have acquired stocks under both names from several different sources over the past 30 years and can find no difference between them. It differs from other mertensias mentioned in having fibrous roots and tufts of green leaves forming a mat of moderate spread. The flowers are borne on tiny spikes and they are of a deep gentian blue shade. This is a plant for shade and it will grow beneath high trees quite well, but it divests itself of foliage in early autumn until early spring. *M. coventryana* has similar growth, but the flowers are purple-blue.

Morina

Another source of interest that comes from a growing knowledge of plants is relationship. A reference book may reveal that some newly-acquired plant belongs to a quite unsuspected family of plants, and this goes for *Morina longifolia*. Its family is *Dipsaceae*, to which scabious also belong and yet there is no superficial resemblance at all. The morina has a long spiny-leaved rosette like a thistle, though green and hairless. It also has a thistly tap root but when the spike of 2 feet or so develops to show the drooping-lipped pink flowers, first impressions vanish. It is a pretty plant and one which seems to have no set season of flowering. A group which will grow quite reliably in sun and any well-drained soil will throw flowering stems on and off all summer, even into

6

November, and if it makes no brilliant display it is a source of interest for a very long time.

Oenothera

Quite often, where annual (or biennial) and perennial species of a genus exist, the former are brighter in flower than the latter, but this could scarcely apply to oenothera. The biennial Evening Primrose lacks the brilliance of several of the perennials, especially the group of dwarf kinds with their large, yellow, saucer flowers, allied to *Oenothera glauca*. These make a clump of massed rosettes with white roots having a distinctive and not unpleasant smell. In June and July they send up twiggy branching stems smothered in long, pointed and sometimes spotted buds which open into large butter-yellow flowers. Under various specific and varietal names like *fruticosa*, *fraseri*, *pilgrimii*, Yellow River and *youngii*, these have been quite popular for a long time but there are a few others of special merit.

The most outstanding of these is *O. cinaeus*. This gives not only a brilliant display of yellow flowers, but some very colourful vernal foliage as well. Once spring growth begins in March, the rosetted leaves take on hues of purple, red, buff and coral. They are some-what spear-shaped, pointing upwards and by May are most attractive. Then in June as the stems run to bud, the colours merge into dark purplish-green, with flowering to cover the next five or six weeks. *O. tetragona* Fireworks (someone deliberately converted its original name of *fyrvekeri* to this) is of similar pattern, but the spring leaf colourings are much less pronounced. *O. glauca* has a few variations, but the most frequently offered is Yellow River. These are all green leaved and yellow flowered, but those with dark or multicoloured foliage have the deepest shades. All grow to about 18 inches with *O. pilgrimii* being rather more stiffly erect, and a new variety named Highlight being especially bright and free flowering. *O. glauca*, by the way, is now the correct name for those formerly classed as *fruticosa*. The latter, of course, signifies shrubbiness, but this could have applied only to the twiggy stems, for the plants themselves are completely herbaceous even if the rosettes retain leaves over winter. All are easy in sun and ordinary soil. In this same category, *O. glabra* should be placed. It differs from the above in having stems less branched, running up to close on 2 feet in good soil. The flowers are large and pure yellow, 2½ inches across.

Oenothera missouriensis dies away to a fangy tap root for the winter and is quite late in making new growth in spring. But given a sunny place and well-drained soil it makes a wide spread of trailing growth during summer, smothering the ground with narrow pointed leaves in which huge light yellow salvers nestle from July to September. Its preference is for a slope over which it can trail and it is too good a plant to confine.

Oenothera acaulis does not spread. The large open yellow trumpets come stemless from a tight rosette of dandelion-type leaves and keep coming for many weeks. This, too, is tap-rooted and prefers dry soil. *O. speciosa* has white, smaller flowers and is quite dwarf; though not long lived, it seeds a little for replenishment.

Omphalodes

The letter 'O' seems to consist of mainly dwarf plants, for the omphalodes are well worthy of inclusion. These and some of the oenotheras are often used as rock garden plants, but omphalodes prefer shade, or if shade is scanty, soil that does not dry out. *Omphalodes cappadocica* has many uses. It can fill a dark corner with dense evergreen foliage or make an edging if one is needed beside a shady path or just as a group where not subjected to blazing sun. In April and May come dozens of little sprays only 6 inches high of tiny but brilliant blue flowers of forget-me-not form. The plants like to be left alone, but if they are divided the early autumn is the best time to do this. This sterling plant has produced a seedling now named after my small daughter Anthea. After trials that began before she was born, this has proved to be even freer to flower and more of a sky-blue shade.

All omphalodes have more or less ribbed leaves, slightly rough to the touch. In *O. lojkae* the leaves are a deeper green and the sprays of blue a little longer and less erect, whilst *O. verna*, with its white variant *alba*, has smaller but broader leaves. Both these root down as they romp in any cool spot, and though dainty make only a brief show of 4-inch sprays in spring.

Orchis

It is sad to see plants which grow happily in the wild taken up and placed in a garden where they stand little chance of survival. People who do this have usually more enthusiasm than knowledge or forethought, for they do not realise that unless such important factors as soil, moisture and aspect are roughly the same in their gardens as where the plants they see are growing naturally, successful transference is unlikely. And if they attempt to move such plants as orchis when in flower, failure is all the more certain and the loss to Britain's dwindling range of choice wild flowers is all the more grievous. It was not until my Dell garden provided conditions of shade and moisture that I decided to try moving an orchis growing wild in a disused lane on the farm, which had deteriorated into a state of bogginess in places, overgrown with thorns and brambles. From the spotted tongue-shaped leaves I guessed the mauvy-purple spikes seen in the little colony to be those of *O. maculata*, and put marker sticks against a score or so. In the following autumn the small claw-like roots, having become dormant, were carefully taken out and planted in the new Dell garden.

They all flowered and to my joy I noticed they were increasing when their second season came. More than this, they grew with stems about 2 feet high and much larger spikes than those in Samson's Lane. After four years, they had become clumps with six or eight spikes each and, as far as I was concerned, were proving very good garden plants indeed. Since then I have tried them both in deeper shade and more open positions and still they flourish and increase. The only special cultivation given them is a topdressing of peat in autumn, and sufficient water to ensure they do not dry out in summer. This success is especially intriguing and satisfying, not only because so few British native orchis are good under cultivation, but because of the variations between them. A few are still dwarf, only about 15 inches high and pale of colour while others run up to more than twice this height in lavender and deep lilac shades, though all flower together from mid June to late July.

This period is a fortnight later than for that superb species, *O. elata*. This is a native of Algeria and I am one of the fortunate few in Britain who appear to have the right conditions for it. A neutral to acid soil, rich in humus, partial shade and no lack of moisture without being boggy, seem to be its main requirements. It sends up leafy stems to over 2 feet in June to carry 6 inches of close-set, lipped flowers of glowing violet-purple.

Perhaps it is rather pointless to rave about plants which are rare
when favourable growing conditions are also rare. *O. elata*, along
with other beauties like *O. maderensis*, is certain always to be
scarce, but I am more hopeful of *O. maculata*. There is confusion
in nomenclature though, and no specialist has given a verdict on
mine. *O. maculata* is known to be variable and is said sometimes to
be confused with *O. latifolia*, which itself may have links with *O.
elata*. As a tailpiece it is worth recording that some plants of my
O. maculata have established themselves happily in the Savill
Gardens at Windsor in a damp grassy place.

Origanum

Plants with aromatic foliage as well as flowering display have a
special appeal but the Marjoram, which is *Origanum vulgare*, has
two interesting variations with scented leaves. The golden-leaved
O. v. aureum is scarcely noticeable in flower but I find it most useful
as a dwarf plant for foliage effect. In my first experimental island
beds of 1953 I placed it in front of the silver-leaved, white-
flowered *Anaphalis yedoensis* and the effect was so pleasing that
these two have remained in company ever since. This origanum
makes dense, mounded, clumpy plants and for eight or nine
months of the year the golden-green is most attractive. Of the
other marjoram variations, I consider both *compactum* and *roseum*
worthy of a place. The former is very compact and ground-cover-
ing, with a sheen of tiny lilac-pink flowers in later summer. *O. v.
roseum* is not quite pink, but the flower heads, rising to 18 inches
above dense, dark green leaves make a pleasing, if subdued display
for many weeks in late summer. These are all vigorous, easy growers.
Pride of place, in my estimation, should, however, be given to *O.
laevigatum*. This has no quickly spreading rootstock, but from a
neat plant there comes an abundance of smooth, slender, wiry
stems set with small glaucous leaves, until by September it bursts
into countless tiny purple flowers like a mist 18 inches high. The
effect is quite striking, and when one pauses to study this very
pretty plant closely, its charm can scarcely fail to appeal.

There are other origanums I wish I could grow with greater
success than has been the case so far. The woolly-leaved *O. hybri-
dum*, with its pinkish hop-like flowers dangling from 12-inch
twiggy sprays, is one of these. Then there is *O. pulchrum*, with

apple-green leaves, and, where happy, an even finer show of drooping 'hops' on 9-inch stems. But these baffle me because plants often rot away in winter, in spite of giving them the extra sharp drainage and sunny positions they are supposed to need.

CHAPTER NINE

Perovskia to Pulmonaria

Perovskias are among the shrubs that are best treated as border perennials. They make 2 to 3 feet of new growth each summer which, in fact, consists of flowering spikes, and for neatness and good effect these are best cut back again every spring to the basal woody shrub, leaving it at about 18 inches high. The leaves are decidedly grey, like sage, and Russian Sage is the common name. The spikes are thin and tapering, and for most of their length a long succession of blue flowers makes for a charming effect in late summer and autumn. The earliest to flower, the lightest blue and the most silvery-leaved is the new variety Blue Mist. This begins in July and the graceful spikes give a brightly ethereal kind of display until well into September. This is one of the best of the many kinds arising from my occasional visits to the Continent. *Perovskia abrotanoides* and *P. superba* appear to be synonymous. Growth is vigorous and the leaves are prettily serrated. The spikes are deep blue but these tend to be a little untidy, and not always self-supporting even though staking would be out of place. *P atriplicifolia* can be like this as a type, but Blue Spire, which flowers from late August to October, is more erect. Another of the combinations I made in 1953 which have become permanent is to have Blue Spire grouped next to the rich orange *Kniphofia galpinii*, and very effective they are together.

Phlomis
Few of the phlomis are exciting. Some are grey-leaved, shrubby plants with heads of yellow flowers. The 2½-foot *Phlomis fruticosa* is the best known of these and is quite useful since it can be planted as a border group. It likes sun and fairly dry soil and can be cut back into shape if it becomes untidy, though it may suffer in very severe winters. *P. chrysophylla* is brighter both in leaf and flower but I find this to be less hardy. The best herbaceous species is

P. samia. This makes a very stout plant with a fair spread of broad, puckered green leaves and sends up a spike set with whorls of light yellow for much of its 4 feet of height in June and July. There is no question of this nor of the pinkish-lavender-flowered *P. tuberosa* being tender. The latter makes a leafy bush 3 feet high, rather lax in rich soil, and in drier soils liable to be rather briefly in flower. *P. viscosa* is interesting, making a greyish-leaved bush 2 feet tall, headed by light yellow flowers for a few weeks around midsummer. None of these phlomis can be regarded as choice but they do possess a modicum of distinction.

Phlox

To pick out just a couple of phlox from among the wide range of varieties existing would appear unjustified but for the fact that the two I mention now are most distinctive. Botanically speaking, *Phlox* Norah Leigh is no more than a variety of *P. paniculata* to which all the popular border varieties belong, and no one would give its flowers a second glance. Its foliage, however, is quite remarkable, and over the past few years it has excited more admiration than any other variegated plant I grow. Even in the new growth appearing in March, the creamy-buff leaves, with just enough green streaks to please the eye, are showy. As it grows upwards in perfect formation, the brightness increases until, by August, well grown plants have reached perfection and a height of about $3\frac{1}{2}$ feet. The pinkish-lilac, crimson-eyed flowers open, adding little or nothing to, nor seriously detracting from, the general picture. Some people prefer to pinch out the budding tips to encourage plants to put all they have into the leaf. To my mind it makes little difference either way, but what does make a difference is to ensure that Norah Leigh is given adequate nutriment and the light soil all border phlox prefer. They do not like heavy clay and if something gritty, with peat or compost can be dug in, then this outstanding plant will hold its foliage until October.

Phlox Norah Leigh, by the way, is not a new variety. It came to me from the owner (after whom it is named) of a Cotswold manor garden who had grown it for over 50 years. Its origin is unknown and though it was believed to have occurred sometime, somewhere in Britain, I was surprised to see a plant in Munich Botanic Garden in 1964 and to be told it had been there for a very long time.

The other distinctive phlox I shall mention is *P. maculata*, a species which produces, not the usual headed truss of flowers but rather whorls of narrow pyramidal formation along 10 to 15 inches of the 3-foot stem. The plants have a more matted spread and less woody rootstock than others, and if anything a longer flowering season. But the colour range is limited to pink and white and it would seem to be another case of neglected development by the hybridist. The brightest pink variety is Alpha, a soft pleasing shade and there is the snow-white Miss Lingard, which is now quite rare. The leaves of these phlox are small, dark green and shiny. The plants are easy to divide and indeed are the better for being divided and replanted in enriched soil every three or four years.

Phygelius
Most of the taller penstemons are lacking either in hardiness or longevity, and beautiful though some are, the whole genus is omitted on this account. The phygelius are quite closely related, but both *Phygelius capensis* and *P. aequilis* are long-lived species, and hardy in spite of some doubts having been laid on the latter score. It is fair enough to claim hardiness for plants which came through the 1963 winter without even the protection of snow, with soil frozen solid to a depth of more than 18 inches. *P. capensis* is a dual-purpose plant. In a sunny bed it sends up 2½-foot spikes widely branched in tiers and dangling scarlet-red tubular flowers. Though it has a long period in flower from early July onwards, there is no massed display at any one time. Light soil and sunshine are certainly appreciated, and sometimes it is grown as a wall plant, secured by netting or trellis. This rather odd alternative method of growing it is possible because, when against a sunny wall, its sub-shrubby nature can develop more fully.

Phygelius aequilis is of a more herbaceous character, though it has similar dark green pointed leaves. The flowers, too, are of similar shape but a little larger and the colour a most unusual suffusion of pale salmon-buff, hanging from arching stems 2 to 2½ feet long. Both species have a quite vigorous spread and are drought resistant.

Platycodon
I have to omit physostegia for though it has the distinctive name

of the Obedient Plant because individual flowers will, if pressed aside from the spike, stay there, this is not in itself sufficient justification for including the genus here. They are quite good garden plants if not left alone so long that they become a nuisance because of the rapid spread of the roots. No such spread, however, occurs with the fleshy-rooted platycodons. With these there is more than the curious distinction of being able to cause a faint explosion when the near-open buds are pinched. These air-filled buds account for the name Balloon Flower, but once open the relationship with Bellflowers is plain to see, even if they are salver- rather than bell-shaped. Platycodons are good value as dwarf plants. None of them grow taller than about 2 feet, and they produce open clusters of 2-inch flowers for several weeks from July to early September. They make a late start from dormancy in spring and one has to be careful not to damage the crowns. They are not fussy about soil and will tolerate a little shade.

Platycodon grandiflorum itself is light blue but a pure white is hard to come by, even if offered as *P. g. album*, and quite often it comes as a very pale blue. There is also a pale pink variety, Mother of Pearl, and semi-double forms occur. The division of these plants is difficult, and as it is usual for plants to be raised from seed they tend to vary a little. The dwarfer *P. g. mariesii* is more widely grown and comes fairly uniformly light blue from seed. The newly introduced *P. apoyama* seems to keep its promise of being 6 inches high for only the first season or two, after which it is as tall as *mariesii*, though the colour is deeper. All platycodons have glaucous leaves coming from the stems and none from the base.

Polemonium

Plants with a short life often have a tendency to seed about in the garden. If these become a nuisance, then one is apt to condemn the genus as a whole instead of just the offending species. The same tendency occurs where certain species are weedy by nature, even if others of the same genus are anything but weedy.

Polygonums are an example of the latter type, but polemoniums, an example of the former, come first. Widely known as Jacob's Ladder, *Polemonium caeruleum* and its variations seed profusely, and self-sown plants appear where they are not wanted, usually after

the parents have ended their short life span of a couple of years or
so. But not all polemoniums are like this. Indeed, the best and
longest-lived species in my garden produces scarcely any seed at
all. This is *P. foliosissimum*. It is a long-lived perennial, with the
pretty leaf formation they all possess — a long midrib with 'steps'
on either side. The flowers are much smaller than those of their
cousins the phlox, but they have the same rounded shape;
they are a warm lavender shade with a yellow eye. Its long
flowering season can be gauged by the fact that a plant from the
group in my garden was sent in flower to the Chelsea Flower Show
in May, 1964, again in July to the Royal Horticultural Society's
Hall, Westminster, and for the third time in August. The reason
for all this was in the hope of it being given an award in recognition
of its qualities, and at the third showing an Award of Merit was
gained. I must admit that it flowered more profusely in 1964 than
ever before in my experience, but it has never failed to make a long
display. The flower heads, on 2½-foot stems, mass together in a
neat upright bush. A much shorter flowering season — in May
and June — does not condemn the variety Sapphire. It is vigorous,
yet neat and long lived and the flowers are light blue, 18 inches tall,
reminding one of Bird's Eye. Blue Pearl is a form of the species *P.
reptans*, a good blue, only 10 inches high and with a tendency to
spread over the surface. *P. lanatum superbum* is pretty, about 18
inches high with quite large mid-blue flowers and a fairly long
season, and there is a compact-growing variety called Pink Pearl
which is dainty and pleasing, though the colour falls short of pink.
This is no more than 12 inches high and flowers from June to
August.

Polygonum
Few genera are more varied as far as form and spread are concerned than the polygonums. From the rank climber of *Polygonum
baldschuanicum* and the handsome but pestilential giant stems of
P. cuspidatum or *P. sachalinense* to the trailing *P. vacciniifolium*,
there are such polygonums as *P. sphaerostachyum* which makes
scarcely any increase at all. I find it an intriguing genus, partly
because of its variety in form and habit. One species, *P. amphibium*,
was growing as a weed in a place that was excavated 4 feet deep to
make a pond. It is still there, growing happily in 3 feet of water and

flowering freely on the surface, whereas it never flowered as a field weed. That is by the way, for it has no place in this context. What has a fully worthy place is the Lowndes form of *P. affine*, which makes a spreading tufty plant with good leaf ground cover and stumpy 8-inch pokers of bright deep pink both in early and late summer. Young plants are in fact seldom out of flower except in early spring when the leaves are mostly brown, till new ones appear. *P. affine* Darjeeling Red is badly named, for this too is a pink. It spreads quickly into wide mats, allowing weeds no chance and gives a long succession of thin deep pink flowers. Any soil will suit these *affine* variations.

Polygonum amplexicaule also has thin pokers, but these come in their hundreds in massed bush formation, 4 feet high. This is a sterling plant, remarkably free to flower and worthy of the space it demands. It makes a massive but compact and somewhat woody rootstock and lasts in flower from July to October. The colour usually seen is deep ruby-crimson, *P. a. atrosanguineum*, but there is a very pale pink *P. a. oxyphyllum* and a fiery salmon-red variety named Firetail of recent introduction. *P. bistorta* as a species is weedy, but the true *P. b. superbum* is well worth growing, especially where the soil is good or a little damp. The leaves are like rounded docks and the 3½-foot spikes carry clear pink poker stripes like thick fingers, in early summer. What has often been listed as *P. bistorta superbum* has now been finally identified as *P. carneum*. This makes a neat leafy plant with no tendency to run, and from late May to July gives a colourful display of bright pink spikes, stumpy in themselves but charming in the mass, about 2 feet tall. As with most polygonums there is a good response to soil which has been enriched and moisture not withheld, but very few polygonums are demanding.

Given dampness, *P. campanulatum* romps away, though it is very pretty with its clusters of pearly flesh-pink flowers on rank-growing stems 3 feet high. This is not a plant for confined spaces, but in dampish wild garden conditions it makes a long and pleasing display. *P. coriaceum* is rare because it is of slow growth, but it is very beautiful. The slender flower spikes 18 inches high are of an intensely clear pink shade, and the leaves are long, dark and crinkly. In the same category comes the true *P. sphaerostachyum*, slow to increase but marvellously free flowering. It has a dense and vigo-

rous summer spread and covers itself in little deep rose spikes
from late May to October, yet it dies back to a comparatively small
rootstock which gives little scope for division. The flowers produce
no seed, at least with me. Both these species are best where there is
moisture, given which they will flower well in both sun and partial
shade.

One of the most outstanding newly-found species of real garden
value is *P. milletii*. This has narrow-tongued leaves of bright green
arising from a smallish rootstock. From it comes a long succession
of pokers on 15-inch stems of an intense shade of red, making a
bright show from June until well into September. So far I have not
dared to try it in a dry, open position, and I fear this would be a
mistake, as I am pretty certain it likes a fair amount of moisture,
though shade may be unimportant.

Polygonum filiforme is not often seen, though it is an easy plant
to grow. It is of somewhat similar habit to *P. amplexicaule*, but
less exuberant, with more rounded, soft-textured leaves, making a
broad bush 3 feet high. From this rise terminal spikes so thin and
needly that the deep brick-red colour makes little impact as a display, but it is an interesting plant none the less. This species seems
to have lately merited a genus of its own and its new name is *Tovara
virginiana filiformis*. There is a very pretty form with variegated
foliage, which, with me, has never flowered, but the foliage alone
is sufficiently attractive for it to be grown. Both are accommodating
and trouble-free, but I find the form *variegata* less vigorous.
Three white-flowered species are also worthy of mention. One is
the 6-inch *P. tenuicaule* which flowers in May. This does not like
dry conditions and it loses vigour if not replanted or mulched
every two or three years. *P. paniculatum*, in contrast, sends up
sturdy, leafy stems 5 or 6 feet tall topped with loose but pretty
sprays in autumn. It wanders slowly below ground but excess
spread is easily curbed. *P. viviparum* has curiosity value, for the
seeds that replace the little off-white flowers on the 15-inch pokery
spikes germinate in situ and drop when ready to take root in the
soil below.

Apart from this, few polygonums are profuse in seed, but one
which I found became a nuisance has, I notice, been recently
offered as a novelty in a seed catalogue. This is *P. capitatum*, having prettily banded leaves, a creeping habit, pale pink flower heads,

a short life and a propensity for seeding itself all over the place. Other polygonums to avoid or to use only as wild garden subjects apart from *P. cuspidatum* and *P. sachalinense* are the rather featureless dwarf white *P. divaricatum* and *P. reynoutria*. The latter is pretty, with good bronzy foliage and creamy-pink flowers. It romps atrociously in some soils, even creeping under obstacles such as paving to find fresh fields to conquer.

Potentilla

I have always nursed a partiality for potentillas and recollect saving up 10*s.* while still a schoolboy with which to purchase one each of a dozen different kinds. This was one of my first ventures in collecting unusual hardy plants but nearly forty years passed before full scope could be given to the urge. Now, with about seventy species and varieties of potentillas in my collection, I must curb my tendency to favouritism and describe only the most garden worthy. Sun lovers all, many will, none the less, tolerate partial shade, but on the whole they are plants for well-drained soil and, for some, excessive richness makes for lush growth at the expense of the flowering display.

Scarcely any attention has been paid to the genus by the hybridists during the past 40 years. Before that there was quite a spate of new varieties and many fine ones originating in France are now rarely seen in cultivation. Perhaps there were too many but of the dozen or more I have of these showy strawberry-leaved varieties, the most outstanding is Glory of Nancy. This has grey leaves, and on the characteristic loose branching stems come almost double flowers quite 2 inches across, of rich crimson and gold flowers from June to August. This reaches 18 to 24 inches as does the flame-orange Wm. Rollisson and the coppery-red Mons. Rouillard. Yellow Queen is dwarfer and silver leaved, and Flambeau and Arc-en-Ciel have red and yellow mottled flowers.

These hybrids probably have *Potentilla argyrophylla* as a parent. This itself has silver leaves carried through winter and in the *atrosanguinea* variation a mass of single scarlet flowers ½ inch or so across is produced in May and June; it is a showy vigorous plant, though rather untidy. The brightest single, longest-flowering red is Gibson's Scarlet, green leaved and lax stemmed, but most effectively brilliant. Pimpernel, about 2 feet tall, is more robust, with larger, glowing red flowers over 1 inch across, but earlier and less continuous. Freedom of flowering, but low marks for longevity, are features of the well-known *P. nepalensis* varieties Miss Willmott, cherry-rose, and Roxana, suffused orange and rose. These reach 20 to 24 inches in height with little basal growth, but though there is plenty of summer spread in Master Floris, I find this prone to die out here and there. This may not be an inherent fault and it would be a pity if this variety, with its trailing sprays of red and primrose flowers over a long period, were to become extinct.

Though all the potentillas mentioned so far would be placed as frontal groups, there are some much dwarfer that are very suitable for small or midget beds. *P. aurea* makes neat green mounds covered in golden flowers and this has a semi-double variation. *P. crantzii* and *P. chrysocraspeda* are on similar lines and there is a pretty warm orange variation of the latter in *aurantiaca*. A vigorous long-flowering white, 6 inches tall, exists in *P. alba*, and *P. fragiformis* bears quite large buttercup-yellow flowers on greyish-leaved plants in May and June.

Taller, and much more erect with yellow flowers more or less on one level at about 2 feet, *P. warrenii* (syn. *P. recta warrenii*) is very pleasing and long flowering. Also erect, the 15-inch high but not very vigorous Glassell's Crimson is deep crimson-red, an uncommon and attractive little plant.

The shrubby potentillas, varieties of *P. fruticosa*, are not out of place among the more herbaceous types. I have a bold group of the beautiful light yellow *P. arbuscula* across a narrow end of an island bed. It has been there for 10 years, a dense mass of silvery-green above close twiggy growth, flowering at least twice each summer by the judicious use of shears to assist the low mounded form, 2 feet high, to keep its shapeliness. This response to pruning or clipping is also made by such deep yellow varieties as Knap Hill and Longacre. *P. fruticosa nana argentea* is silver leaved and naturally dwarf, and the white-flowered *P. f. mandshurica* keeps under 2 feet in height. It would be a mistake to place any of these shrubby kinds where they could be overhung or hemmed in by taller plants.

Pulmonaria

If peonies and pyrethrums must be omitted from this book so must

the vast range of primulas. When compiling a hardy plant catalogue as most nurserymen do every year, there is always some relief
to reach the end of the letter 'P', including, as it does, such long
lists of species and varieties to be described and priced. But this is
no catalogue, and my objective selectiveness has to be maintained.
But one more subject before 'P' is left must be included, and it is
one variation of that quite common spring-flowering plant, the
pulmonaria or Lungwort. In my estimation *P. angustifolia azurea* is
a real treasure for all its easy growth. In March, it bursts forth with
new leaves and semi-prostrate sprays of the most intense blue
flowers imaginable, at their best in April. This is a shade-loving
plant, but not the least fussy about soil. If too close to trees it will
make less of a show but this only means that it responds to
reasonable treatment and the somewhat fleshy-rooted plants are
not likely to die even if it becomes very dry during the summer
that follows. This also applies to *P. saccharata*. This is coarser
growing and scarcely to be recommended except the variety called
Pink Dawn which has handsome, spotted ash-green leaves that
give good ground cover and dangling pink bells, which appear in
early spring.

Right: The true *Macleaya cordata* is a rare plant, with a haze of tubular white flowers, reaching a height of about 6 feet

Left: The brilliant scarlet flowers of *Lychnis arkwrightii* are well set off by the darkly purple leaves

Right: *Mertensia virginica* has translucent blue trumpets in the spring, lasting for several weeks

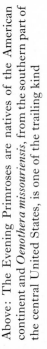

Above: The Evening Primroses are natives of the American continent and *Oenothera missouriensis*, from the southern part of the central United States, is one of the trailing kind

Right: A superb stand of *Orchis elata* growing in the author's garden; its glowing violet-purple flowers appear in June

CHAPTER TEN

Ranunculus to Veronica

For some, gardening is a case of filling space with what is easiest to grow, if they bother at all. This method may involve one or more specialities from roses to rock plants or from annuals to shrubs according to preference or suitability for soil and situation. Hardy plants, however, embrace such a wide diversity that a selection could be made that would grow in any given soil or situation found in English gardens. When enthusiasm reaches the pitch of wanting to grow plants not fully adaptable to one's particular soil then gardening becomes a challenge, and when this challenge is accepted, successes bring the savour of triumph along with mounting interest and widening knowledge. To reach that happy state, one has to have both a love and a 'feeling' for plants and experience may have been gained partly by trial and error. Losses as well as successes with rare or uncommon plants may well have occurred, but this is an integral part of one's gardening life.

My own experiences include a fair number of failures, in spite of having unusually favourable conditions since I went all-out to collect and grow uncommon plants. The vast majority of them grew well, just as they would in most gardens, but what I find especially satisfying is the ease with which so many choice plants grow once their basic needs are met. An example is *Ranunculus aconitifolius flore-pleno*, the double, white Fair Maids of France. This has been in sparse cultivation for generations, but for years I shied away from trying it again, having lost it the first time. The Dell garden, with places for both moisture and shade lovers, led me to try it once more in moist, sandy loam in full sun and there it has flourished ever since. Double white flowers do not appeal to everyone, but this, somehow, is different for in each there is perfection of form and composition and in May and June a group becomes a 2-foot mound of dark green foliage studded by countless numbers of these intensely white buttony flowers $\frac{1}{2}$-inch or so across. The roots are fingery, from a quite small central crown, and dormancy during autumn and winter is complete. As for adaptability, this is wider than I had imagined and it seems fairly safe to say that where its relative the trollius will thrive, so will this charming ranunculus.

Another double, but bright yellow in this case, will grow in any sunny situation, but it is by no means choice. This is *R. acris flore-pleno*, flowering at about the same time and with much more resemblance to the Buttercup. This grows quite erectly to 2½ feet. *R. gramineus*, as its name denotes, is grassy leaved, the glaucous green leaves radiating from a neatly growing plant. Stems 9 to 12 inches high carry glistening yellow flowers for several weeks and make this an attractive little plant for the front of a sunny bed or border.

Rhazya (and Amsonia)

One of the seeming anomalies in plant nomenclature is to place *Amsonia* and *Rhazya* as separate genera. I have heard some people aver that *Amsonia tabernaemontana* and *Rhazya orientalis* are identical but though there is a difference, the two may just as well come together here. *A. tabernaemontana salicifolia* has slender willow-leaved stems 2 feet or so tall borne in great profusion from a tough, sturdy but compact root. For several weeks, small light blue flowers of periwinkle form make a pleasingly graceful plant, but no bright display. *R. orientalis* grows more compactly, with smaller darker leaves and the deeper blue flowers are more closely clustered. Both plants are easy to grow in any sunny or half shady place, yet in spite of having considerable charm, both remain uncommon.

Rheum

Just as the culinary rhubarb is of easy culture, so is the rarely seen ornamental species *Rheum palmatum*. Its fault is that of being too massive for most gardens, and because its leaf spread is vast, there is a considerable gap when these die back in late summer. Where space permits, however, the magnificence of its early summer display, with statuesque spikes up to 8 feet high in May and June, is a sight to behold. The type is pink flowered, but deeper, almost red shades come in the *atrosanguineum* and *rubrum* forms. An early attraction lies in the new spring growth, which in March and April is highly coloured in pinks, red and purple. Even taller, but a little later is the variety *tanguticum*. This has a tinge of bronze in the deeply lacinated leaves and more than a tinge in its towering, tapering spikes.

Rodgersia

No garden with a moist shady place should be without one or more of the rodgersias. It would be superfluous to go much beyond a passing mention because few gardens have moist shade and rodgersias need room to show their beauty. Most of the half dozen or so species have handsome green or slightly bronze foliage some-what like giant chestnut leaves in shape, but carried as umbrellas to about 3 feet high. Above come pretty creamy-white plumes in July to give a charming effect. *Rodgersia aesculifolia*, *R. purdomii*, *R. podophylla* and *R. pinnata* are on these lines, but the finest by far is the bronzy-purple-leaved, pink-flowered *R. pinnata superba*. Then there is the flatter, umbrella-leaved *R. tabularis*, with shiny colourful tinges and creamy-white flowers. Rodgersias are easy, hardy and quite trouble-free just so long as they can stay with roots damp and leaves sheltered from strong sun and wind.

Roscoea

The roscoeas are still quite rare in gardens yet they are reasonably adaptable, as well as rather fascinating. The roots are fleshy and lie deeply in the soil and they are one of the tardiest of plants to poke through in spring. Until the winter of 1963 proved their hardiness for me, doubts often arose on this score when I found no sign of new shoots as late as mid May. Yet each year, the final emergence about that time is followed by a remarkably swift development and in about a month they are in full flower.

The flowers of roscoeas are curiously shaped, akin both to a large-lipped lobelia and to some orchids, and the leaves are stem clasping and speary. The earliest to appear and flower is *Roscoea cautleoides*, primrose-yellow and about 20 inches high. A variation, *R. c. beesii*, has yellow and violet-purple shadings, and is of similar height without the fault of self seeding that some have, especially the pretty violet-purple-flowered *R. purpurea*. *R. alpina* is a soft lilac-pink shade but dwarfer at 9 inches. This, too, seeds itself, but this is not so much of a fault because there is no wide dispersal of seedlings, though I once ran into trouble when, in ignorance of this propensity, I moved out a group of *R. cautleoides* and replaced it with *R. purpurea*. The result was a chaotic mixture of both, for the young plants are hard to find when dormant. I find roscoeas grow happily in sun or partial shade so long as not starved of moisture and nutriment during the May–August period of growth and flower, but plants should be set a good 6 inches below ground.

Rudbeckia
One often sees old borders of the conventional style all too narrow for the tall plants placed at the rear, where the backing makes them taller and weaker still. One has either to look up to see the flowers, if staking has been adequate, or lacking this, they are to be seen lolling over in an unsightly fashion, harmful to any lowlier plants within reach of their ungainly stems. The tall rudbeckias are usually to be seen in such borders, *Rudbeckia laciniata* or *nitida* in double or single varieties like Golden Glow or Herbstsonne. Though my garden is large I have no place there for these lanky 6- to 8-footers which will not stand up unaided. I wish, however, that there existed a dwarfer, more erect, single-flowered variety, as companion to the charming double Goldquelle, which makes a neat, upstanding, leafy bush only 3 feet tall. The colour is chrome-yellow and it lasts in flower from August to October. *R. subtomentosa* is single flowered but this has light grey-green hairy leaves, and stiff 3-foot stems bearing deep yellow, black coned flowers in late summer. It is an easy, robust plant, but fades rather quickly in starved conditions. This applies to the deservedly popular Black-eyed Susan, from the amazingly free *R. deamii* at 2½ feet, the fairly common *R. speciosa* (syn. *R. newmanii*) to the rich orange-yellow of *R.* Goldsturm, which is only 20 inches tall and flowers for 10 to 12 weeks from late July to October. The last-mentioned is a first-rate plant.

Rudbeckia purpurea, the purple Coneflower, is sometimes listed under *Echinacea*. This, for all its basically magenta colouring, seldom fails to attract, with its rayed petals hitched to an upstanding black, gold-tinged cone, atop rigidly branching stems from 2½ to 3½ feet tall in later summer. It is variable in the sense that a purchase as plain *R. purpurea* would probably not be all exactly

Above: Norah Leigh is a striking variegated-leaved variety of phlox

Below: *Platycodon grandiflorum*, the Balloon Flower, pops open its inflated flower buds of light blue from July until the autumn

Above: Pink spikes of flowers and deeply cut palmate leaves are the characteristics of this ornamental rhubarb, *Rheum palmatum*

Right: Moist shady places suit the rodgersias; here *R. podophylla* lifts its plumy white flowers in the shade of light woodland

alike, and sometimes a hybrid strain is offered, as are a few named varieties. Of these The King is most widely grown and it has large purplish-magenta flowers on 3½-foot stems which are not always self supporting. The new Robert Bloom is a little shorter, of much neater bush formation and the flowers are broader petalled, of a warmer shade in which rose-red is more dominant than purple-magenta. This is the result of many years selective work in which the colourful but less vigorous *R. purpurea* Abendsonne was used for breeding, but the new variety lacks nothing in vigour and free-dom in flower. White Lustre, of American origin, tends to grow on one, once accepted for what it is worth. It is not startlingly white and it has an orange cone, a good habit and a long season in flower.

Salvia

There are dozens of species of hardy salvias, seen only in collectors' or botanic gardens. Some are quite pleasing, but having tried out a good many, if I had to cut down garden space, several would have to go. In other words, not many are fully deserving as garden plants and here only the best can be included. The best, without any doubt, are the variants of *Salvia superba*, which itself should never be left out of a collection of top-line subjects. Its long suc-cession of deep violet spikes on sturdy 40-inch bushes with greyish leaves will grace any bed or border. In recent years dwarfer varieties have arrived to widen the scope of this species, but the general picture and purpose is the same. The variety Lubeca is 2 to 2½ feet tall, a little earlier and a trifle more blue than *superba*, while East Friesland is only 15 to 18 inches and a grand little plant for a frontal group. More recently still May Night (or Mai Nacht) has come. This, too, is dwarf and begins to flower in late May, continuing for weeks on end with new spikes poking through others that have faded. At least this happens with the young plants I have grown, but it may, as do many border perennials, tend to flower more profusely over a shorter period when more fully established. All these salvias are easy in almost any soil, preferring sun but not minding partial shade. *S. haematodes* is good but, with me, not so permanent, though I have heard of plants living for many years in some gardens. In any case a few self-sown seedlings appear as replenishments to a group, which makes a fine sight in June and July. The flowers are individually larger than the *superba* varieties and of a light lavender-blue shade carried on sturdy 3-foot spikes.

If the sky-blue *S. uliginosa* were stronger stemmed, a little earlier flowering and hardier, it would be a very valuable plant indeed. But lax growth 4 feet tall, October flowering and sometimes January dying, make it of value only to those in mild districts who do not mind the staking chore. *S. ambigens* is reputedly tender, but here at Bressingham it has come through sub-zero temperatures protected only by a low mound of leaves. It is erect as a 4-foot bush of bright green leaves on which there is a long if sparse, succession of clear blue flowers on short spikes.

Satureia and Scabiosa

A word in here for *Satureia montana caerulea* for a frontal position. This makes a low green bush of dense greenery and in late summer is covered in tiny blue flowers that make a most pleasing effect. A word, too, for *Scabiosa graminifolia* as a sterling plant for the front of the border. It has pretty narrow silvery leaves of year-round value and makes a display of lilac-mauve pincushions that lasts for three months from June to September and is only 10 inches high.

Sedum

Some of the sedums are very good border perennials. The Ice Plant type, *Sedum spectabile*, is not uncommon and is very good value, especially in the deeper pink varieties such as Carmen or Meteor which in September attract bees and butterflies as well as the human eye. The new hybrid Autumn Joy is fast becoming as popular as it deserves to be. Growth is a little taller and more robust at 2 feet on established plants, and it is effectively glaucous all through the summer until, in September, the wide plate heads begin to open into flower. At first pale rose, these change to a salmon shade when fully open and, always changing, always attractive, they fade into russet brown by November. Ruby Glow is rosy-red and reaches only 10 inches or so when in August the heads of flower in bluish foliage are fully open. This is the period when two other sedums come into flower. Both *S. roseum* and *S. telephium* Redcap are green leaved by comparison with those already mentioned, the first being nearly 2 feet tall and Redcap about half that height. *S. maximum* has one fine variation in the purple-leaved *S. m. atropurpureum*, grown for its fine foliage. This, too, has wide heads of flower, but these are rather nondescript in colour. *S. caucasicum* has robust growth and good foliage and its flower heads of a sulphur-buff shade are of considerable charm, flowering at 2 feet in September. All these sedums are easy in any well-drained soil, preferring a mainly sunny position and needing the minimum of attention over a period of several years.

Some of the new varieties raised at Bressingham have come about by sheer luck, either as a selection from a batch of seedlings or in one or two cases from a seedling that appeared by chance. This element of luck is always present. The greater the diversity of plants grown, and the more appreciative one is of plants, the more likely the chances of a find. Deliberate crossing, breeding or hybridising holds a fascination for many gardeners. It appeals not only to creature instincts but to acquisitive instincts as well, and I am not the only one to have indulged in fanciful notions about making a small fortune and perhaps some fame from some new plant. Now I know better, having learned the hard way. I would in fact go so far as to say that if the time and effort put into raising new varieties over the past 35 years had been spent in producing larger quantities of existing kinds that sell readily, I would have been financially a good deal better off.

But no matter. The most important factor has now become that of raising new plants which will enhance the range of good garden subjects. To achieve this one has to be fairly objective. One must perceive a need for a plant of given height or colour and then, if the species or genus lends itself to variation, one sets about the task of building with patience and determination. Success is never assured and the odds are usually heavily against a break. Hundreds of seedlings raised, scores of selections made and trials carried out over several years are still no guarantee of final success, but perseverance is usually rewarded in the fullness of time, in one way or another.

Sidalcea
Success came fairly quickly with sidalceas. I had asked Percy Piper, who does the 'fiddling' as he calls breeding, if he would try to produce some dwarf varieties of this graceful plant. Most of those

in cultivation being on the tall side and apt to need staking, here was the need. Two years later Percy had a couple of hundred seedlings in flower. From these, in another two years, from the first selection made, three very pleasing plants were being tried out as garden groups. And now, three years later still, they have just been launched as Puck, Oberon and Titania. All are in shades of light or clear pink, 2, 2½ and 3 feet in height respectively, and so shapely and strong of habit as to be impervious to high winds. They arose, incidentally, from a very fine parent, the little known variety Mrs Alderson, with large clear pink flowers on shapely spikes 4 feet high. Sidalceas are easy to grow in almost any soil, but prefer sun to make their little mallow salvers glisten during July and August.

Stachys

Stachys now include plants we used to know as *Betonica*, which is rather a pity because the latter has the more pleasant name. *Stachys macrantha* (formerly *Betonica grandiflora*) is a very good garden plant, making a shapely bush of stippled leaves and neat spikes up to 2½ feet tall, with deep rosy-lilac lipped flowers. This is a bright, good-natured plant that should always be included in a bed or border where freedom from trouble is important. *S. densiflora* is dwarfer and of a brighter, decidedly pink colour. The spikes are stumpy and close together to make a pyramid about 18 inches high encircled by sizeable bright green leaves. It has a long flowering period from June to late August, is easy to grow in any sunny position, and can be left alone for several years. There is a pure white form with an equally long, if not longer, flowering period, but since it grows to only 9 to 10 inches it must have a frontal position. *S. officinalis nana* has flowers of that purple-rose shade which some people dislike but it is a very effective little plant. Good foliage, stubby spikes to 12 inches, and again a long flowering season from July to September make this a subject not to be despised. I consider it quite admirable.

Stokesia

The stokesia or Stoke's Aster has a closer kinship, when the flower is studied, with cornflowers than asters. The plants have dark green, leathery, tongue-shaped leaves carried quite close to the ground, and through these come smooth stems branching a little to carry disproportionately large flowers from July until September. Heights vary from 9 to 18 inches and though blue is decidedly the dominant colour, none are a pure shade but are suffused with pink and with some white in the centre. Blue Star is very fine, with flowers 3 inches across, but what is offered as the type, *S. laevis* (*S. cyanea*), is somewhat smaller and dwarfer. In reasonable soil and a sunny place with good drainage, stokesias are first rate plants.

Thalictrum

One of the most interesting genera, with species varying in height from 3 inches to 7 feet, is thalictrum. They all have pretty foliage and one, *Thalictrum minus adiantifolium* is called the Hardy Maidenhair. Almost without exception they are best in deep, fairly rich soil that does not suffer drought severely, and though several are decidedly robust, one or two demand a fair amount of fussing if favourable conditions are not ready-made in a garden. The earliest to flower of those in cultivation is *T. aquilegifolium*. The name describes the glaucous leaves, which stand out from the stiff $3\frac{1}{2}$-foot stems. By late May the branching heads are about to open with clouds of rounded puffs of mauve-purple, but in about a month the display has ended. Variations of this colour are not wide. Purple Cloud and Thundercloud are much the same and Dwarf Purple is no more than 3 feet. There is, however, the white *T. a. album*, I like this very much and it is more striking, especially in partial shade or against a background of shrubs. These are easy, reliable plants to grow, as are the yellow-flowered thalictrums of the *glaucum* type, which ascend to a good 5 feet and more in moist soil. *T. flavum glaucum* itself, together with *T. rugosum* and *T. sphaerocephalum*, has blue-grey foliage, straight stems and cloudy heads of fluffy flowers in June and early July. *T. flavum* is green leaved, and there is a variety named Illuminator which has a golden hue in the foliage before spikes are formed. The best of these green-leaved, yellow-flowered thalictrums is *T. angustifolium*. The foliage is dark and shiny, the stems straight and strong to 6 feet and the flowers nearer yellow than the others. All are variations of sulphur-yellow, but with me *angustifolium* is brighter, later by a week or two and holds its colour longer.

Among the choicest of plants for humus soil in cool shade is the entrancing *T. diffusifolium* (which has also been known as *T. diffusiflorum*). I tried it for several years in more open positions without success and now it is happily suited; the display it gives of violet-mauve, yellow-centred flowers on very prettily foliaged bushes 18 inches high, is most rewarding, from late June until well into August. The plants are tiny and rather frail and one wonders how so much can come from so little. Yet it is perfectly hardy and perennial for all its lack of increase. I find that much the same conditions are best for *T. dipterocarpum* Hewitt's Double and this, too, makes but little growth below ground. But Hewitt's Double will grow in more open situations so long as the soil is deep, light, fairly rich and does not dry out. This, too, makes a pretty maidenhair-leaved bush to about 2½ to 3 feet but it is inclined to loll and become tangled with its neighbours. The flowers are perfectly formed, soft mauve-blue and mostly cover the mid-July to early September period. *T. dipterocarpum* itself will not stand unaided and it may run to 6 feet in rich soil. This is a very pretty plant for those who do not mind staking or untangling the thin, twiggy stems if they wish to use some for cutting. This species, too, has an attractive white variation. It is not so tall nor so robust and the foliage is a light apple-green shade.

Thalictrum minus includes some rather nondescript variations, the only one of garden value being *T. m. adiantifolium*, the so-called Hardy Maidenhair. The flowers are greenish and very tiny, but the foliage, on bushes about 2½ feet high, is pretty for a long time. This is very easy to grow in sun or partial shade and does not mind dry soil. Another very good thalictrum responsive to good treatment but otherwise easy and adaptable, is *T. rochebrunianum*. From a hefty rootstock come very long stems, powdered and grey-blue with leaves to match on widely held stalks. Height may vary from 3 to 6 feet, according to the moisture available, and in June come quite large lilac-pink flowers on branching sprays. This is the kind of plant that has grace and beauty as well as sturdiness and it ought to be more widely grown.

Thermopsis and Tiarella
I must mention only briefly such uncommon perennials as *Thermopsis lanceolata* and *Tiarella polyphylla* and *T. trifoliata*. *Thermopsis lanceolata* should be included for it is bright and early,

rather like a yellow lupin about 3 feet tall and at its best in late May. It is uncommon, I believe, because no one seems to have bothered with it, but I find it well worth growing in a sunny place. Garden worthiness also applies to two of the shade loving tiarellas. Both *Tiarella polyphylla* and *T. trifoliata* have tiny, ivory-white flowers in sprays 12 inches high, but the former are rather pearl-like in shape, whereas the latter are open and misty looking. Both make close-growing, well-foliaged plants of good ground cover value, and though more responsive to a cool position they will not languish where conditions are on the dry side. They flower for a long time.

Tovara

The plant until recently known as *Polygonum filiforme*, is now *Tovara virginiana filiformis*, but I have described it with the polygonums (see p. 93).

Tricyrtis

Moistish shade suits *Tricyrtis stolonifera*, one of the little known Toad Lilies. This makes a spread of matted roots, and stems grow leafily to 2 feet or so to produce a long succession of trumpets $1\frac{1}{2}$ inches across of a pale lilac shade, delicately marked and spotted crimson within. This is a plant one needs to pause by to appreciate, for it makes no bright display. What it does is to add interest to a shady, moist corner for many weeks in later summer, for it possesses a curious beauty.

Valeriana

Much more imposing than the flowers of *Tricyrtis stolonifera* are the wide umbels of *Valeriana sambucifolia*, consisting of hundreds of tiny flesh-pink flowers. From strongly growing plants with elder-shaped leaves, dark and shiny, stems grow to four feet or more. In good soil these are a trifle vulnerable to high winds, but as a background or in the lee of some break, it is a pleasing plant to grow for the June-July period. And for something like it in miniature there may be more room for *V. arizonica*. This only reaches 6 to 8 inches with little heads of palest pink in May and June.

Vernonia

Back to something tall and to the back end of the season, the vernonias are worth mentioning. These, too, have plate-heads of flowers, each flower being by way of a puff of stamens glowing richly crimson-purple in the autumn sun, for they do not open until October has come. The stems are strong and straight, with narrow speared leaves all the way up to 5 feet or so in the case of *Vernonia crinita*. *V. noveboracensis* is not quite so tall, nor are the heads so wide but the colour is the same. The plants are compact and may be left alone for years, being easy to grow in any mainly sunny situation.

Veronica

It is hard to think of any genus so widely diverse as *Veronica*, even apart from the many shrubby kinds now called *Hebe*. From one or two that are scarcely more than a film of greenery over the soil, to the tall spiky species that make for such welcome variation in a border, few are without charm or interest. It will be best if I deal with veronicas in groups, according to height.

Veronica gentianoides comes within those that grow under 2 feet in height and it is one of the earliest to flower. It makes mats of fresh green leaves and by early May the spikes of light blue are beginning to open with typical Bird's-eye flowers. This is an easy plant in sun or shade and if the show is not for long, the compensation is in its early brightness. There is a dwarfer variation, growing up to 12 inches, and a variegated-leaved form of this, as well as a seldom seen white. Not long after come the intensely blue *V. teucrium* varieties, which make a magnificent show in June. Shirley Blue is 9 inches tall, Crater Lake Blue a little deeper and an inch or two taller, with *V. t. amethystina* and Royal Blue at 18 inches or so. The new variety Blue Fountain reaches 2 feet and flowers a week or two later. All these veronicas produce short but massed spikes in somewhat lax bush formation when established, from matted fibrous roots. If the plants are spaced 9 inches apart they will more or less join as a solid group in about three years. All are quite easy in any reasonable soil.

Veronica spicata makes surface mats of foliage from which spikes arise more erectly than those of the *teucrium* type even if the individual flowers are small. The flowers come from June to

Above: The porcupine
cones of *Rudbeckia
purpurea* White Lustre
are orange, and are
surrounded by long
narrow white petals

Right: *Sedum roseum* is
the Rose Root, with fleshy
leaves and greenish-
yellow flowers in August

Above: *Stokesia laevis* Blue Star is a particularly good form with flowers 3 inches across in late summer

Right: An extremely distinctive veronica, *V. longifolia subsessilis hendersonii*

August, and the spikes are mostly between 1 and 2 feet high. *V. spicata incana* and Saraband have spikes of violet-blue. The latter is more free to flower, but, while both are grey leaved, *incana* is the lighter shade. The variety Wendy is similar, but its spikes at nearly 2 feet have a tendency to loll. Pink shades include Minuet, a pretty little plant with greyish leaves and 15-inch spikes, and Barcarolle is a deeper shade of pink, green leaved, and growing to about 20 inches. Romiley Purple is violet-blue, 2 feet tall and green leaved. Two dwarf veronicas of merit which are almost unknown are the light blue, 1½-foot *V. androsovskyana*, semi-mat forming and flowering freely from July to autumn, and *V. grandis* which makes little 15-inch spiky bushes much earlier in summer. Finally in this group comes the most distinctive *V. longifolia subsessilis hendersonii* with pointed foliage and making dense and darkly green mounds up to 12 or 18 inches. From these come 6-inch spikes like those of a violet-blue buddleia, pointing outwards rather than upwards. This is a choice plant for later summer and one that I myself find somewhat baffling. It makes a wide mass of fibrous roots, and when it decides to grow makes a fine show. But in spite of changes of soil, I find it dies away sometimes, quite inexplicably, and I have not yet found a spot where the early promise that it will be fully suited is maintained.

Veronica longifolia itself grows up to 3 feet. As with the *V. teucrium* varieties, summer growth dies completely, leaving no surface growth during winter. *V. longifolia* is pretty, with upward tapering spikes but it is apt to be untidy and weak stemmed. I do not rate either this or the white form very highly, but *V. exaltata*, which may be a sub-species, is in a different class. Stout plants of matted fibrous root send up 4-foot stems, brightly green with pointed leaves and fine mid-blue spikes in August and September. In open beds it should not need staking, but it might do so if the soil is moist and the plants are hemmed in. Standing supreme in my estimation among the taller veronicas is *alba*, the white form of *V. virginica*. This variety needs no staking for the stems are very strong, even if sometimes they attain 6 feet. The leaves are arranged symmetrically in whorls at 4- to 6-inch intervals for two-thirds of the stem, the rest being the slender but imposing flower spikes which fit in so well with the late July and August border pattern. For some reason the blue *V. virginica* is less attractive and makes a briefer display, and this applies to the pale pink variety *rosea* as well, though both have the same pleasing gothic form. All these tall kinds are of easy culture — but responsive none the less to nutriment — and are adaptable to either sunny or half-shady positions.

CHAPTER ELEVEN

Plants for Special Purposes

It will be understood that the lists which follow do not include all
the kinds of plants suitable for the purposes stated. To avoid
complications, only those plants mentioned in this book are placed
in the various categories, these serving as a guide to those who
might prefer to make a selection in keeping with the 'distinctive'
plants described. Other books by myself give further information
for those wishing to learn of other perennials suitable for specific
soils and situations.

The descriptive glossary should be used in conjunction with the
index to obtain the fullest information on the plants classified for
special purposes. These lists are given merely as introductions to
the kinds of plants that may meet particular needs and it should
not be assumed that all the species and varieties of the genera
listed are suitable.

FOR DRY SHADE

Anaphalis
Crambe
Epimedium
Euphorbia
Geranium
Omphalodes
Polygonum

GOOD OVERALL APPEARANCE AND SHRUB ASSOCIATION

Acanthus
Achillea — dwarfer kinds
Alchemilla
Amsonia
Anaphalis
Anemone japonica
Arnebia
Artemisia
Asphodeline
Aster
Astrantia — where not dry
Campanula
Centaurea
Chelone
Chrysogonum, where not limy
Cimicifuga — where not dry
Crambe
Crocosmia
Cynara
Dicentra

Dictamnus
Epimedium
Eryngium
Eupatorium
Euphorbia
Geranium
Gypsophila
Helleborus — where not dry
Hemerocallis
Heuchera
Heucherella
Hosta
Jurinea glycacantha
Kniphofia
Lavatera
Liatris
Linum
Liriope
Macleaya
Malva
Mertensia
Morina
Oenothera
Perovskia

Phlomis
Phlox
Phygelius
Polemonium
Polygonum
Potentilla
Pulmonaria
Rhazya
Rheum
Rudbeckia — dwarfer kinds
Salvia
Satureia
Scabiosa
Sedum
Sidalcea
Stachys
Stokesia
Thalictrum — erect kinds
Thermopsis
Tiarella
Tricyrtis — where not dry
Valeriana
Vernonia
Veronica

WINDY AND EXPOSED

Achillea — dwarfer kinds
Alchemilla
Anaphalis
Anemone japonica
Artemisia
Aster — dwarf kinds
Centaurea
Chelone
Coreopsis
Dictamnus
Eryngium
Gentiana — *septemfida* and
   allied species

Geranium
Gypsophila
Hemerocallis
Heuchera
Jurinea
Kniphofia
Lavatera
Liatris
Linum
Lychnis
Malva
Oenothera
Origanum

Platycodon
Polygonum — dwarf kinds
Potentilla
Rudbeckia — dwarf kinds
Scabiosa

Satureia
Sedum
Stokesia
Veronica

FOR TOWN GARDENS

Alchemilla
Amsonia
Anaphalis
Anemone japonica
Aruncus
Asphodeline
Aster
Astilbe
Astrantia
Calamintha
Campanula
Chelone
Chrysogonum
Cimicifuga
Coreopsis
Crambe
Dicentra
Epimedium
Eryngium
Eupatorium
Euphorbia
Filipendula
Gentiana
Geranium
Heliopsis
Helleborus
Hemerocallis
Heuchera
Heucherella
Hosta
Incarvillea

Kirengeshoma
Liatris
Ligularia
Linum
Liriope
Lychnis
Lysimachia
Macleaya
Mertensia
Morina
Oenothera
Omphalodes
Phlomis
Phlox
Platycodon
Polemonium
Polygonum
Pulmonaria
Rhazya
Rheum
Roscoea
Rudbeckia
Salvia
Satureia
Sedum
Sidalcea
Stachys
Thalictrum
Tiarella
Tricyrtis

FOR CHALKY SOIL

Acanthus
Achillea
Alchemilla
Alstroemeria
Anaphalis
Anemone japonica
Artemisia
Asphodeline
Aster
Astrantia
Calamintha
Campanula
Centaurea
Chelone
Cimicifuga
Coreopsis
Crambe
Crocosmia
Cynara
Dicentra
Dictamnus
Epimedium
Eryngium
Euphorbia
Filipendula
Geranium
Gypsophila
Heliopsis
Helleborus
Hemerocallis
Heuchera
Hosta
Incarvillea
Jurinea

Kniphofia
Lavatera
Liatris
Ligularia
Linum
Lychnis
Lysimachia
Macleaya
Malva
Mertensia
Oenothera
Omphalodes
Origanum
Perovskia
Phlomis
Phygelius
Platycodon
Polemonium
Polygonum
Potentilla
Pulmonaria
Rheum
Rudbeckia
Salvia
Satureia
Scabiosa
Sedum
Sidalcea
Stachys
Stokesia
Thalictrum — most kinds
Thermopsis
Veronica

MOISTURE-LOVING AND WATERSIDE

Astilbe
Aruncus

Astrantia
Dierama

Eupatorium
Filipendula
Hosta
Ligularia
Lysimachia

Orchis
Polygonum
Ranunculus
Rodgersia
Thalictrum

SILVER OR VARIEGATED

Achillea Moonshine
Achillea clypeolata
Anaphalis
Artemisia (except *lactiflora*)
Centaurea — most kinds
Cynara
Eryngium — some kinds
Euphorbia — some kinds

Hosta — some kinds
Origanum — some kinds
Perovskia
Phlomis — some kinds
Phlox Norah Leigh
Pulmonaria — some kinds
Scabiosa graminifolia
Sedum — some kinds

CUT FLOWER

Achillea
Alstroemeria
Asphodeline
Astilbe — taller kinds
Astrantia
Campanula — taller kinds
Centaurea
Cimicifuga
Coreopsis — some kinds
Crocosmia
Eryngium
Gentiana asclepiadea
Gentiana axillariflora
Gypsophila — taller kinds
Heliopsis
Helleborus
Heuchera
Heucherella

Hosta
Jurinea
Kniphofia
Liatris
Lychnis — taller kinds
Lysimachia — taller kinds
Macleaya
Polygonum — taller kinds
Ranunculus
Roscoea
Rudbeckia — some kinds
Sidalcea
Stachys — taller kinds
Stokesia
Thalictrum
Thermopsis
Valeriana

HEAVY OR CLAY SOIL

Achillea filipendulina and others
Alchemilla

Amsonia
Aster — most kinds

Astrantia
Calamintha
Centaurea
Coreopsis
Crambe
Epimedium
Eupatorium
Filipendula
Gentiana — summer-flowering
    kinds
Geranium
Heliopsis
Helleborus — some kinds
Hemerocallis
Hosta
Ligularia
Lychnis
Lysimachia
Macleaya

Mertensia
Oenothera — most kinds
Omphalodes
Orchis — where moist
Phlomis
Platycodon
Polemonium
Polygonum — most kinds
Potentilla
Pulmonaria
Ranunculus — most kinds
Rhazya
Rheum
Rodgersia — where moist
Rudbeckia
Salvia — most kinds
Sidalcea
Stachys
Valeriana

DROUGHT-RESISTANT IN SUN

Acanthus
Achillea — dwarfer kinds
Alstroemeria
Amsonia
Anemone japonica
Artemisia
Asphodeline
Aster — some kinds
Campanula — most kinds
Centaurea
Chelone
Coreopsis
Crocosmia
Cynara
Dictamnus
Eryngium
Euphorbia
Gypsophila

Heliopsis
Heuchera
Incarvillea
Jurinea
Kniphofia
Lavatera
Liatris
Lychnis — some kinds
Linum
Liriope
Malva
Morina
Oenothera — some kinds
Origanum
Perovskia
Phlomis
Phygelius
Platycodon

Polemonium
Polygonum — some kinds
Potentilla
Rhazya
Salvia
Satureia

Scabiosa
Sedum
Stokesia
Thermopsis
Veronica — some kinds

SHADY WHERE NOT DRY

Alchemilla
Anemone lesseri
Astilbe
Astrantia
Calamintha
Campanula — some kinds
Chrysogonum
Cimicifuga
Dicentra
Dodecatheon
Epimedium
Eupatorium
Euphorbia — some kinds
Filipendula
Gentiana — some kinds
Geranium — most kinds
Helleborus
Hemerocallis

Heucherella
Hosta
Kirengeshoma
Lysimachia
Macleaya
Mertensia
Omphalodes
Orchis
Phlox — some kinds
Polygonum — most kinds
Pulmonaria
Rodgersia
Roscoea
Salvia
Thalictrum
Tiarella
Tricyrtis
Valeriana

GOOD FOLIAGE FOR GROUND COVER

Alchemilla
Artemisia
Centaurea
Dicentra — some kinds
Epimedium
Euphorbia
Geranium — most kinds
Helleborus — some kinds
Heuchera
Heucherella
Hosta

Liriope
Omphalodes
Origanum — some kinds
Polygonum — some kinds
Potentilla — some kinds
Pulmonaria
Satureia
Sedum — some kinds
Tiarella
Veronica — some kinds

CHAPTER TWELVE

Merit List and Plant Index

Any guide to merit should take account of such attributes as constitution, longevity, annual spread, erectness of habit, duration of flowering season and adaptability. The last-mentioned is the most difficult to assess, because many plants are worthy of full marks only if given perfect conditions. Nearly all the astilbes, for example, are in this category. Given moisture and a little shade, they fulfil all other requirements for top marks, but if deprived of these conditions they fall sadly short. Marks are therefore given with this fully in mind, with very few if any deductions made because of lack of adaptability to conditions they do not like. It would be a mistake for any reader to make a selection of those with the highest ratings and expect them all to grow to perfection together in one bed or border. Full information on requirements is given for those plants which are not very adaptable.

Plants with no claim to garden worthiness are given no marks at all. If some have only half the merit ratings of others it does not mean that they are only half as worthy. It means that in my own experience they are less valuable on one score or another and the references to the descriptive section of the book will reveal the reasons for rating variations.

SPACING GRADES

It will be seen that many of the numbers given for planting density leave room for discretion. Such factors as soil fertility, natural or applied, and economics are chiefly concerned. Where soil is known to be rich or to promote good growth through no lack of moisture, then the smallest of the recommended numbers of plants to plant to the square yard will suffice. But if cost does not count greatly and a quick response is more important, then the larger number of plants given for the square yard can be planted. This closer spacing should, of course, apply in less fertile soil, but for the sake of economy, the lesser number could be used, bearing in mind that it would take longer — one season or possibly two — for the bed or border to become fully established. In any case, the lower planting density where variations of a plant or two per square yard are given, could scarcely fill out before the end of the first season after planting, especially if planting is not completed until spring. It must also be emphasised that the planting numbers per square yard are given on the assumption that plants of good or reasonable quality are used, such as one could expect to obtain from a reliable retailer. It would be worth the little trouble involved to make quite sure on this point in advance of ordering a quantity, although the majority of plants recommended in this book could only be obtained from hardy plant specialists who could be relied upon to send out good-quality stock.

Merit List and Plant Index

MERIT MARKS 1 TO 10		PLANTS PER SQUARE YARD	PAGE REF.
10	*Acanthus longifolius*	3 to 4	27
8	*mollis*	3 to 4	27
6	*perringii*	5 to 6	27
10	*spinosus*	3 to 4	27
6	*spinosissimus*	5	27
8	*Achillea clypeolata*	5	28
8	*filipendulina*	4	27
10	Moonshine	4 to 5	28
8	*taygetea*	5	28
8	*Alchemilla mollis*	4 to 5	28
8	*Alstroemeria ligtu* hybrids	5 to 6	29
8	*Amsonia tabernaemontana salicifolia*	4 to 5	98
8	*Anaphalis margaritacea*	4	29
8	*nubigena*	5	29
8	*pterocaulon*	4	30
8	*triplinervis*	5	29
8	*yedoensis*	4	30, 85
10	*Anemone hupehensis* September Charm	6	31
10	*splendens*	6	31
10	*japonica* Bressingham Glow	6	30
10	Kriemhilde	5	30
10	Lady Mary Gilmour	5	30

MERIT MARKS		PLANTS PER	PAGE
1 TO 10		SQUARE YARD	REF.
	Anemone—cont.		
10	Louise Uhink	5	30
10	Max Vogel	5	30
10	Montrose	5	30
10	Profusion	6	30
10	Queen Charlotte	5	30
10	Whirlwind	5	30
8	*lesseri*	6 to 7	31
8	*Arnebia echioides*	5	31
6	*Artemisia argentea*	4	32
6	*baumgartenii* (syn. *A. villarsii*)	3 to 4	32
6	*discolor*	4	32
9	*lactiflora*	4	33
6	*ludoviciana*	3 to 4	32
9	*nutans*	5	33
6	*palmeri*	3 to 4	32
6	*pontica*	3 to 4	32
6	*purshiana*	3 to 4	32
8	*splendens*	4	32
6	*stelleriana*	3 to 4	32
9	*Aruncus sylvester*	4	35
8	*Asphodeline liburnica*	4 to 5	32
8	*lutea*	4 to 5	32
8	*Aster acris*	4 to 5	33
8	*nanus*	5	33
6	*cordifolius*	4 to 5	34
10	*frikartii*	5	34
8	*laevis*	4 to 5	34
8	*linosyris*	5	34
8	Goldcrest	5	34
8	*spectabilis*	4 to 5	34
8	*thomsonii*	5 to 6	33
7	*Astilbe astilboides*	4 to 5	35
9	Bonn	4 to 5	35
9	Bressingham Beauty	4	36
9	Cattleya	4	36
8	*chinesis pumila*	4	36
9	Coblence	4 to 5	35
9	Cologne	4 to 5	35
8	*crispa* Perkeo	5	36

MERIT MARKS 1 TO 10		PLANTS PER SQUARE YARD	PAGE REF.
8	*Astilbe davidii*	4	35
9	Deutschland	4 to 5	35
9	Dusseldorf	4 to 5	35
9	Fanal	4 to 5	36
9	Federsee	4 to 5	36
8	Finale	4 to 5	36
9	Fire	4 to 5	35
8	*glaberrima saxosa*	7 to 8	36
9	Glow	4 to 5	35
9	Irrlicht	4 to 5	36
9	Ostrich Plume	4	36
8	Red Sentinel	4 to 5	35
9	Rheinland	4 to 5	35
7	*rivularis*	3 to 4	35
8	Salland	4	35
7	Salmon Queen	3 to 4	35
8	*simplicifolia*	5	36
9	*atro-rosea*	5	36
9	Bronze Elegance	6	36
9	Dunkelachs	5	36
9	Spinell	4 to 5	36
8	Tamarix	4	35
9	*taquetii superba*	4	35
7	Venus	3 to 4	35
8	*Astrantia major*	4 to 5	36
9	*maxima*	4 to 5	37
8	*rubra*	5 to 6	37
	Betonica see *Stachys* (p. 132)		
	Bocconia see *Macleaya* (p. 128)		
7	*Calamintha grandiflora*	4 to 5	39
9	*nepetoides*	4 to 5	39
9	*Campanula alata*	4 to 5	41
7	*alliariifolia*	4 to 5	41
8	*burghaltii*	4 to 5	42
10	*carpatica*	6 to 7	40
6	*glomerata*	4	41
8	*acaulis*	5	41
6	*dahurica*	4 to 5	41
8	Joan Elliott	5	41
8	Purple Pixie	6 to 7	41
9			

MERIT MARKS		PLANTS PER	PAGE
1 TO 10		SQUARE YARD	REF.
	Campanula—cont.		
8	*superba*	4 to 5	41
10	*lactiflora*	4 to 5	40
10	Loddon Anna	4 to 5	40
10	Pouffe	4 to 5	40, 41
10	Prichard's Variety	5	40
8	*latifolia*	4 to 5	41
8	Brantwood	4 to 5	41
8	Gloaming	4 to 5	41
9	*latiloba* Percy Piper	4 to 5	41
8	*trachelium* Bernice	5	42
8	Van Houttei	4 to 5	42
6	*Centaurea dealbata*	4	42
8	*steenbergii*	4	42
9	John Coutts	4	42
7	*glastifolia*	4 to 5	42
9	*hypoleuca*	5	43
8	*macrocephala*	3 to 4	42
6	*montana*	4	42
8	*orientalis*	4 to 5	43
8	*pulchra major*	4	43
8	*ruthenica*	5	42
7	*simplicicaulis*	5	43
8	*Chelone barbata*	5	43
7	*lyonii*	5	44
8	*obliqua*	4 to 5	43
6	*alba*	4 to 5	44
8	*Chrysogonum virginianum*	5 to 6	44
9	*Cimicifuga cordifolia*	4 to 5	44
9	*dahurica*	4 to 5	44
9	*japonica*	4 to 5	44
10	*racemosa* Elstead Variety	4 to 5	44
10	White Pearl	4 to 5	44
9	*ramosa*	4	45
9	*Coreopsis grandiflora* Goldfink	5	45
9	Rotkichlen	5	45
9	*verticillata*	4 to 5	45
10	*grandiflora*	4 to 5	45
6	*rosea*	4 to 5	45
8	*Crambe cordifolia*	3 to 4	46

MERIT MARKS 1 TO 10		PLANTS PER SQUARE YARD	PAGE REF.
10	*Crocosmia masonorum*	8 to 10	46
8	*Cynara scolymus*	3 to 4	47
10	*Dicentra* Adrian Bloom	5	50
9	Bountiful	5	50
8	*eximia*	4 to 5	49
8	*alba*	5	49
10	*spectabilis*	4	48, 49
9	*Dictamnus fraxinella*	5	50
8	*Dodecatheon*	7 to 8	50
9	*Epimedium grandiflorum*	4 to 5	52
9	*perralderianum*	4 to 5	52
9	*pinnatum*	4 to 5	52
9	*colchicum*	4 to 5	52
9	*rubrum*	4 to 5	52
9	*warleyense*	4 to 5	52
9	*youngianum*	4 to 5	52
9	*niveum*	4 to 5	52
9	*roseum*	4 to 5	52
8	*Eryngium alpinum*	5	53
8	*amethystinum*	4 to 5	53
9	*bourgatii*	5 to 6	53
7	*bromeliifolium*	4	52
8	*dichotomum*	5	53
7	*giganteum*	4 to 5	53
8	*leavenworthii*	5	53
7	*maritimum*	6 to 7	53
8	*oliverianum*	4 to 5	53
7	*pandanifolium*	4	52
7	*planum*	5	53
7	*serra*	4	52
8	*tripartitum*	5	53
8	*variifolium*	4 to 5	53
8	Violetta	4 to 5	53
9	*Eupatorium purpureum*	4	53
8	*rugosum*	4	53
8	*Euphorbia biglandulosa*	4 to 5	55
8	*characias*	4	54
10	*epithymoides*	4 to 5	54
8	*griffithii*	4 to 5	54
10	Fireglow	4 to 5	55

MERIT MARKS 1 TO 10		PLANTS PER SQUARE YARD	PAGE REF.
	Euphorbia—cont.		
8	*myrsinites*	4 to 5	55
8	*palustris*	4	55
8	*sikkimensis*	4	55
8	*wulfenii*	4	54
7	*Filipendula digitata*	5	57
8	*nana*	5	57
8	*elegantissima*	4 to 5	57
7	*gigantea* (syn. *F. camtschatica*)	4	57
9	*hexapetala plena*	5	57
7	*palmata*	5	57
8	*purpurea* (syn. *F. palmata rubra*)	5	57
8	*rubra* (syn. *F. venusta magnifica*)	4	58
9	*Gentiana asclepiadea*	5	58
8	*axillariflora*	5	58
9	*bisetaea*	6 to 7	58
9	*doeringiana*	6 to 7	58
9	*hascombensis*	6 to 7	58
8	*lagodechiana*	6 to 7	58
8	*makinoi*	5	58
9	*septemfida*	6 to 7	58
10	*latifolia*	6 to 7	58
9	*sino-ornata*	9 to 10	59
10	*Geranium armenum*	4	59
9	*cinereum* Ballerina	6 to 7	61
9	*subcaulescens*	5 to 6	61
8	*dalmaticum*	6 to 7	61
8	*endressii* A. T. Johnson	4	59
8	Rose Clair	4	59
8	Wargrave Pink	4	59
8	*farreri*	6 to 7	61
8	*grandiflorum*	4	59
9	*ibericum*	4 to 5	59
10	Johnson's Blue	4 to 5	59
7	*macrorrhizum*	4 to 5	59
7	*phaeum* and *p. lividum*	4 to 5	61
9	*pratense album plenum*	5	60
9	*coeruleum plenum*	5	60
9	*purpureum plenum*	5	60

MERIT MARKS 1 TO 10		PLANTS PER SQUARE YARD	PAGE REF.
9	*Geranium renardii*	5 to 6	60
8	*sanguineum*	4 to 5	60
10	Holden Variety	4 to 5	60
10	*lancastriense splendens*	4 to 5	60
8	*sylvaticum* Mayflower	5	61
9	*wallichianum* Buxton's Blue	5	61
8	*wlassovianum*	5	61
9	*Gypsophila paniculata*	3 to 4	61
8	Bristol Fairy	3 to 4	61
9	*compacta plena*	3 to 4	62
7	Flamingo	3 to 4	61
9	Pink Star	4 to 5	62
8	Rosy Veil	4 to 5	62
9	*Heliopsis scabra gigantea*	4 to 5	62
10	Golden Plume	5	62
9	Goldgreenheart	5	62
9	*patula*	5	62
9	*incomparabilis*	5	62
9	*Helleborus atrorubens*	5	63
8	*corsicus*	4 to 5	63
8	*lividus*	5	63
9	*orientalis*	4 to 5	63
8	*sternii*	5	63
8	*viridis*	5	63
9–10	*Hemerocallis* Black Magic	4 to 5	64
9–10	Doubloon	4 to 5	64
9–10	Felicity	4 to 5	64
9–10	Golden Orchid	4 to 5	64
9–10	Hyperion	4 to 5	64
9–10	Larksong	4 to 5	64
9–10	*middendorffii*	4 to 5	64
9–10	*minor*	4 to 5	64
9–10	Morocco Red	4 to 5	64
9–10	*multiflora*	4 to 5	64
9–10	Pink Damask	4 to 5	64
9–10	Pirate's Treasure	4 to 5	64
9–10	Primrose Mascotte	4 to 5	64
9–10	Salmon Sheen	4 to 5	64
9–10	Stafford	4 to 5	66
8	*Heuchera* Bloom's Variety	5	65, 66

MERIT MARKS 1 TO 10		PLANTS PER SQUARE YARD	PAGE REF.
	Heuchera—cont.		
9	Bressingham Blaze	5	66
9	Bressingham Hybrids	5	66
8	Carmen	5	66
8	Firebird	5	66
8	Freedom	5	66
8	Ibis	5	66
9	Scintillation	5	66
8	Sparkler	5	66
8	Splendour	5	66
9	*Heucherella* Bridget Bloom	5 to 7	66
10	*Hosta albomarginata*	4 to 5	68
10	*crispula*	4 to 5	68
10	*fortunei*	3 to 5	67
10	*albopicta*	3 to 4	68
10	*robusta*	3 to 4	67
8	*lancifolia*	4 to 5	67
8	*fortis*	3 to 5	67
9	*plantaginea*	4 to 5	67
10	*rectifolia*	3 to 4	67
10	*sieboldiana*	4 to 5	67
10	*elegans*	3 to 4	67
8	*tardiflora*	5 to 6	67
10	Thomas Hogg	4 to 5	68
10	*undulata medio-variegata*	4 to 5	68
10	*ventricosa*	3 to 4	67
10	*aureo-variegata*	3 to 4	68
8	*Incarvillea* Bees' Pink	5 to 6	69
8	*delavayi*	5 to 6	69
8	*grandiflora*	6 to 7	69
8	*Jurinea glycacantha*	4 to 5	69
8	*Kirengeshoma palmata*	3 to 4	70
9	*Kniphofia* Ada	4	72
9	Alcazar	4	72
9	Bees' Lemon	4	72
9	Bees' Sunset	4	72
9	Buttercup	4	72
7	*caulescens*	3 to 4	71
10	*galpinii*	4 to 5	70, 71
9	Gold Else	4	72

MERIT MARKS 1 TO 10		PLANTS PER SQUARE YARD	PAGE REF.
9	*Kniphofia* Goldmine	4	72
9	*macowanii*	4 to 5	71
10	Maid of Orleans	4	72
9	*modesta*	4 to 5	72
9	*nelsonii*	4 to 5	71
9	Royal Standard	4	72
8	*rufa*	4 to 5	71
10	Samuel's Sensation	3 to 4	72
9	Springtime	4	72
9	*tubergenii*	4	71
7	*tuckii*	3 to 4	71
8	Underway	4	72
9	Yellow Hammer	4	72
9	*Lavatera olbia rosea*	3 to 4	73
9	*Liatris callilepis*	5 to 6	73
8	*graminifolia*	5 to 6	73
9	Kobold	5 to 6	73
7	*pycnostachya*	5 to 6	73
9	*Ligularia clivorum* Desdemona	3 to 4	74
8	Gregynog Gold	3 to 4	74
8	Othello	3 to 4	74
8	*hessei*	3 to 4	74
8	*hodgsonii*	4 to 5	74
7	*marcrophylla*	3 to 4	75
8	*przewalskii*	4	74
9	The Rocket	4	75
7	*smithii*	3 to 4	75
8	*stenocephala*	3 to 4	75
8	*veitchiana*	4 to 5	75
8	*wilsoniana*	3 to 4	75
7	*Linum austriacum*	5 to 6	75
8	*campanulatum*	5	75
9	*dolomiticum*	5	75
8	*flavum*	5 to 6	75
9	*narbonnense*	5 to 6	75
9	*gentianoides* and Six Hills	5 to 6	75
9	*paniculatum*	5 to 6	75
6	*perenne*	5 to 6	75
7	*tenuifolium*	5 to 6	75
8	*Liriope* Majestic	5	76

MERIT MARKS 1 TO 10		PLANTS PER SQUARE YARD	PAGE REF.
	Liriope—cont.		
10	*muscari*	5	76, 77
8	*spicata*	5 to 6	76
8	*Lychnis arkwrightii*	6 to 8	77
8	*chalcedonica*	4 to 5	77
9	*coronaria*	4 to 5	77
8	*dioica* Emneth	4 to 5	77
9	Red Admiral	4 to 5	77
8	*flos-jovis*	6 to 7	77
8	*haageana*	6 to 8	77
9	*viscaria splendens flore-pleno*	6 to 7	77
9	*Lysimachia clethroides*	4 to 5	78
8	*ephemerum*	4 to 5	78
8	*punctata*	3 to 4	78
7	*vulgaris*	3 to 4	77
10	*Macleaya cordata*	4 to 5	79
8	*microcarpa*	4 to 5	79
9	Coral Plume	4 to 5	80
9	*Malva alcea fastigiata*	4 to 5	80
8	*Mertensia ciliata*	5	80
7	*coventryana*	5 to 6	81
8	*echioides* (or *M. primuloides*)	5 to 6	81
7	*paniculata*	5	80
9	*virginica*	5 to 6	80
8	*Morina longifolia*	4 to 5	81
8	*Oenothera acaulis*	5 to 6	83
10	*cinaeus*	5	82
9	*glabra*	5 to 6	82
8	*glauca*	5	82
10	Highlight	5	82
10	*missouriensis*	4 to 5	83
9	*pilgrimii*	5	82
7	*speciosa*	5 to 6	83
9	*tetragona* Fireworks	5	82
9	Yellow River	5	82
10	*Omphalodes* Anthea Bloom	5 to 6	83
10	*cappadocica*	5 to 6	83
9	*lojkae*	5 to 6	83
7	*verna*	4 to 5	83
9	*Orchis elata*	5 to 6	84, 85

MERIT MARKS 1 TO 10		PLANTS PER SQUARE YARD	PAGE REF.
9	*Orchis latifolia*	5 to 6	85
9	*maculata*	6 to 7	84, 85
9	*maderensis*	5 to 6	85
8	*Origanum hybridum*	6 to 7	85
10	*laevigatum*	6 to 7	85
8	*pulchrum*	6 to 7	85
8	*vulgare aureum*	4 to 5	85
8	*compactum*	4 to 5	85
8	*roseum*	4 to 5	85
9	*Perovskia abrotanoides*	4	87
8	*atriplicifolia*	4	87
10	Blue Spire	4	87
10	Blue Mist	4	87
8	*Phlomis chrysophylla*	3 to 4	87
7	*fruticosa*	3 to 4	87
8	*samia*	4	88
7	*tuberosa*	4	88
7	*viscosa*	4	88
8	*Phlox maculata* Alpha	4 to 5	89
8	Miss Lingard	4 to 5	89
8	*paniculata* Norah Leigh	4 to 5	88
8	*Phygelius aequilis*	4	89
8	*capensis*	4	89
9	*Platycodon apoyama*	5 to 6	90
9	*grandiflorum*	5	90
9	*album*	5	90
9	*mariesii*	3 to 6	90
9	Mother of Pearl	5	90
6	*Polemonium caeruleum*	5	90
9	*foliosissimum*	5	91
8	*lanatum superbum*	5	91
7	Pink Pearl	5	91
8	*reptans* Blue Pearl	5	91
8	Sapphire	5	91
8	*Polygonum affine* Darjeeling Red	3 to 5	92
10	Lowndes Variety	4 to 5	92
10	*amplexicaule atrosanguineum*	3 to 4	92
10	Firetail	3 to 4	92
8	*oxyphyllum*	3 to 4	92
9	*bistorta superbum*	4 to 5	92

MERIT MARKS 1 TO 10		PLANTS PER SQUARE YARD	PAGE REF.
	Polygonum—cont.		
8	*campanulatum*	3 to 4	92
10	*carneum*	4 to 5	92
8	*coriaceum*	4 to 5	92
6	*divaricatum*	4 to 5	94
	filiforme variegata (see *Tovara*, p. 132)		
9	*milletii*	5 to 6	93
8	*paniculatum*	3 to 4	93
9	*sphaerostachyum*	5	92
6	*tenuicaule*	5 to 6	93
6	*reynoutria*	3 to 4	94
7	*Potentilla alba*	5	95
10	*arbuscula*	4	95
8	Arc-en-Ciel	4 to 5	94
8	*argyrophylla*	4 to 5	94
8	*atrosanguinea*	4 to 5	94
8	*aurea*	5 to 6	95
8	*chrysocraspeda*	5 to 6	95
8	*aurantiaca*	5 to 6	95
8	*crantzii*	5 to 6	95
8	Flambeau	4 to 5	94
7	*fragiformis*	5 to 6	95
9	*fruticosa* Knap Hill	4	95
9	Longacre	4	95
9	*mandshurica*	4	95
9	*nana argentea*	4	95
10	Gibson's Scarlet	4 to 5	94
8	Glassell's Crimson	5 to 6	95
10	Glory of Nancy	4 to 5	94
9	Mons. Rouillard	4 to 5	94
8	*nepalensis* Master Floris	4 to 5	95
8	Miss Willmott	5	95
9	Pimpernel	4 to 5	94
8	Roxana	5	95
8	*warrenii* (syn. *P. recta warrenii*)	4 to 5	95
10	Wm. Rollisson	4 to 5	94
9	Yellow Queen	4 to 5	94
10	*Pulmonaria angustifolia azurea*	5	96
8	*saccharata* Pink Dawn	5	96

MERIT MARKS 1 TO 10		PLANTS PER SQUARE YARD	PAGE REF.
9	*Ranunculus aconitifolius flore-pleno*	5	97
8	*acris flore-pleno*	4 to 5	98
8	*gramineus*	5 to 6	98
8	*Rhazya orientalis*	4 to 5	98
8	*Rheum palmatum atrosanguineum*	3	98
8	*rubrum*	3	98
8	*tanguticum*	3	99
8	*Rodgersia aesculifolia*	4	99
8	*pinnata*	4	99
10	*superba*	4	99
8	*podophylla*	4	99
8	*purdomii*	4	99
8	*tabularis*	4	99
7	*Roscoea alpina*	6 to 7	99
8	*cautleoides*	5 to 6	99
8	*beesii*	5 to 6	99
8	*purpurea*	6 to 7	99
10	*Rudbeckia deamii*	4 to 5	100
6	Golden Glow	3 to 4	100
10	Goldquelle	4 to 5	100
10	Goldsturm	4 to 5	100
6	Herbstsonne	3 to 4	100
8	*purpurea*	5	100
8	Abendsonne	5	101
10	Robert Bloom	5	101
9	The King	5	101
8	White Lustre	5	101
9	*speciosa* (syn. *R. newmanii*)	4 to 5	100
8	*subtomentosa*	4	100
8	*Salvia ambigens*	4	102
9	*haematodes*	5	101
10	*superba*	4 to 5	101
10	East Friesland	5	101
10	Lubeca	4 to 5	101
10	May Night	5	101
7	*uliginosa*	4	102
8	*Satureia montana caerulea*	5	102
10	*Scabiosa graminifolia*	5	102
8	*Sedum caucasicum*	4 to 5	103
9	*maximum atropurpureum*	5	103

MERIT MARKS I TO IO		PLANTS PER SQUARE YARD	PAGE REF.
	Sedum—cont.		
8	*roseum*	4 to 5	102
10	*spectabile* Autumn Joy	4 to 5	102
10	Carmen	5	102
10	Meteor	5	102
10	Ruby Glow	4 to 5	102
8	*telephium* Redcap	4 to 5	102
8	*Sidalcea* Mrs Alderson	4 to 5	104
9	Oberon	5	104
9	Puck	5	104
9	Titania	5	104
9	*Stachys densiflora*	5	104
9	*macrantha*	4 to 5	104
9	*officinalis nana*	5 to 6	104
10	*Stokesia* Blue Star	5	105
8	*laevis* (syn. *S. cyanea*)	5	105
8	*Thalictrum angustifolium*	4	105
8	*aquilegifolium album*	5	105
8	Dwarf Purple	5	105
8	Purple Cloud	5	105
8	Thundercloud	5	105
8	*diffusifolium*	6 to 7	106
8	*dipterocarpum*	4 to 5	106
9	Hewitt's Double	5	106
7	*flavum*	4	105
7	*glaucum*	4	105
8	Illuminator	4	105
7	*minus adiantifolium*	4 to 5	105
8	*rochebrunianum*	4	106
8	*T. rugosum*	4	105
7	*sphaerocephalum*	4	105
8	*Thermopsis lanceolata*	4 to 5	106
8	*Tiarella polyphylla*	5	106
8	*trifoliata*	5	106
7	*Tovara virginiana filiformis variegata*	4	93, 107
8	*Tricyrtis stolonifera*	5	107
8	*Valeriana arizonica*	6 to 7	107
8	*sambucifolia*	4 to 5	107
9	*Vernonia crinita*	4	108
8	*noveboracensis*	4	108

MERIT MARKS 1 TO 10		PLANTS PER SQUARE YARD	PAGE REF.
8	*Veronica androsovskyana*	5	109
9	*exaltata*	4	109
8	*gentianoides*	4 to 5	108
8	*grandis*	5 to 6	109
7	*longifolia*	4 to 5	109
9	*subsessilis hendersonii*	4 to 5	109
9	*spicata* Barcarolle	5	109
8	*incana*	5	109
9	Minuet	5	109
8	Romiley Purple	5	109
9	Saraband	5	109
9	Wendy	4 to 5	109
9	*teucrium amethystina*	4 to 5	108
10	Blue Fountain	4 to 5	108
10	Crater Lake Blue	5	108
9	Royal Blue	4 to 5	108
10	Shirley Blue	5	108
8	*virginica*	4	109
10	*alba*	4	109
8	*rosea*	4	110

General Index

Note: Plant names are excluded from this Index. References to these will be found in the Merit List and Plant Index, pages 119–133.

botanical names, 37–8

chalky soil: plants for, 114
clay soil: improving, 14
  plants for, 115–16
colour in display, 12
compost, 14
continuity of flowering, 16
cut flowers: plants providing, 115

display: planting for, 12
drainage, 13
drought: plants resistant to, 116–17

exposed positions: plants for, 112–13

fence: disadvantages of, behind border, 10
flowers, cut: plants providing, 115
foliage: for ground cover, 117
  silver or variegated, 115

ground cover, 117
grouping of plants, 14–15, 17

hedge: disadvantages of, behind border, 10
herbaceous border: converting to island bed, 13, 20
  disadvantages, 10
  making best of, 13
  planning, 17
  positioning, 10
humus, 14

island bed, 13
  advantages, 10, 14
  conversion from border, 13, 20
  planning, 14, 17
  planting, 15
  shape, 14
  size, 14

manuring, 14
moisture-loving plants, 114–115

name changes, 37-8
nomenclature, 37-8

peat, 14
perennials: form, 15
  interest shown in, 9
  planting, 18-19
  planting time, 18
  selecting, 15
plan: drawing up, 16, 17
planting methods, 17-18
plants: form, 15
  grouping, 14-15, 17
  height, in relation to width of
    bed, 17-18
  positioning, 15-16
  selecting, 15
  spacing, 17, 118-19
  for special purposes, 111-17

sand, sharp, 14
shade: planting, 20-21
  plants for, 20, 111, 117

shrubs: herbaceous plants to
    associate with, 111-12
  in mixed border, 21-2
site preparation, 13
soil: feeding, 14
  plants for different types, 114,
    115-16
spacing of plants, 17, 118-19
staking, 21
sun: plants for, 116-17

town gardens: plants for, 113
turf: digging in, 14
  moving, 14

wall: disadvantages of, behind
    border, 10
waterside: plants for, 114-15
weeds, 13
wind: plants resistant to, 112-
    113
woodland: conditions in, 22
  plants for, 117